MAKING YOUR
BUSINESS
GOD'S
BUSINESS

To Nancy, my wife and best friend.
I can't imagine life without her!

What you are about to read is how the Lord
worked in my life, but none of this would
have happened without Nancy by my side.
She has been an encouragement and support
throughout all aspects of my life.

"Jeff's inspirational story and experienced wisdom gives you a road map to success in business—God's way! This book is a must-read for every Christian business owner and leader who desires greater impact for Christ with their business, their influence and their life."

—PASTOR GREG JOYNER, president, R3 Ministries

"A real life story that should inspire us all to trust the faithfulness of Jesus in all of life, especially business. Jeff's example enlightens you to see how your business offers amazing eternal opportunities!

—MERLE STOLTZFUS, Stoltzfus Enterprises Ltd.

"A firsthand description of a life of faith in God and joy in giving. What a combination! Anyone who reads this fun but challenging book will be refreshed by Jeff's candor, simple faith, and global vision.

—DR. ANDREW BUNNELL, CEO, Biblical Ministries Worldwide

"Buckman is the mentor Christian businesspeople need! The chapters of this book read like eight coaching sessions over coffee, full of spiritual wisdom and practical business know-how."

—DR. DAVID HOSAFLOOK, missionary and missions historian

MAKING YOUR BUSINESS GOD'S BUSINESS

Having a front row seat to watch God use your business to impact the world

JEFF BUCKMAN

CEO of Buckman's, Inc.

Making Your Business God's Business: Having a front row seat to watch God use your business to impact the world

© Jeff Buckman, 2020

ISBN 978-1-946244-98-7

Editing and book design: David Hosaflook

IAPS (Longwood, FL)

Publishers-in-Publication Data:

Name: Buckman, Jeff

Title: Making Your Business God's Business: Having a front row seat to watch God use your business to impact the world

ISBN 978-1-946244-98-7 (paperback)
ISBN 978-1-946244-99-4 (e-book)

Subjects (BISAC): REL063000 RELIGION / Christian Living / Stewardship & Giving | REL045000 RELIGION / Christian Ministry / Missions | BUS046000 BUSINESS & ECONOMICS / Motivational

Library of Congress Control Number: 2020914070

CONTENTS

ACKNOWLEDGMENTS

I would like to thank two people who encouraged me to write and finish this book. Without them it simply would not have been completed.

The first is Pastor Greg Joyner. He would know just the right time to ask, "How is that book coming? The story needs to be told!" Or he would say something like "Other business people need to know this and apply what you have learned to their business practices." As we all know, there are tons of things to accomplish every day, so writing this book kept getting pushed to the bottom of my to-do list. Pastor Joyner's promptings would spur me on to tackle another chapter!

The second is David Hosaflook, a missionary to the Albanian people. Our friendship started with a mission trip back in 2006. David is an excellent writer. Without his editing and cover design—and many, many suggestions along the way—the book wouldn't have been completed. Many thanks to both Pastor Joyner and David!

WHY WRITE A BOOK?

"Who, me? Write a book? I don't think so!"

That was my response when my evangelist friend said, "Buckman, you need to write down what you do so others can learn and do the same thing."

This evangelist and I have long been friends and co-laborers in various projects over the years. Through him, I learned of a seminary in Puerto Rico that needed some equipment to video record classes. At my friend's suggestion, I helped the seminary obtain that equipment. The impact of that gift was more than I expected: the videos have been used all over the world in training Spanish-speaking seminary students!

When my friend challenged me to put down on paper the things that the Lord was doing in my heart—and through my business (Buckman's, Inc.)—I said I would start writing and show him the draft in a year. The year came and went, and my small draft didn't really cover much.

In addition to my evangelist friend, one of the pastors at our local church has mentioned to me many times, "Jeff, you need to write your story down. Get it on paper so others can learn from it!" At first, I answered that there really isn't anything special about my story—just a Christian business guy trying to serve the Lord with what He has given me.

Time and time again the pastor would nudge, "How's that book coming? What chapter are you on now? Keep at it. Tell your story so others can learn from it and do the same thing!"

The Lord was just not letting me get away from this!

The final call to action came when my wife and I had the opportunity to take three couples on a ski vacation. Two of the couples serve the Lord as missionaries in foreign countries, and the third directs a Christian camp here in the States. We went to Zermatt, Switzerland, and had a wonderful time of fellowship, along with many discussions about each of their ministries, and—of course—skiing. Through my business we have had many opportunities to support each of these ministries. The giving budget of the business has funded building projects, flights for them or their children to and from the mission field, computers and other equipment, and many special projects. Rest assured, these couples are a few who have observed how the Lord has used Buckman's Inc. in ministry.

On the last night of that ski trip, the three couples sat my wife and me down before dinner and said, "Jeff, you need to take seriously writing a book. What you do in using your business around the world for ministry isn't done by many other Christian businessmen." They even threw into the conversation that they thought it was *the Lord's will* for me to write a book, and that the Lord could use the book in a mighty way as others read it and begin to use their businesses to help ministries.

So here I am, writing a book in hopes that other Christian businesspeople will learn something from what I have learned over the past forty-five years (and counting)! By doing this, they may be able to "fast track" to being used of the Lord in a greater way, and will not have to spend decades learning the way I did. Perhaps others can see how they can use their businesses for the Lord and His work locally and around the world. I hope that others will catch the vision that their businesses are part of God's plan to make an eternal difference!

I want others to see that they can go to the Lord for direction about how to run their businesses. In my experience, God blesses that which is yielded to Him, and He has directed me in business decisions.

I want others to see, also, that they can have both a ministry and a business, and how rewarding both can be! People living and serving in this way will be blessed far beyond their wildest dreams! They will discover new relationships and see friendships formed that last not only for a lifetime, but for eternity. It truly has been an awesome life that I want others to experience.

BEGINNINGS

My Salvation Testimony

I think it is important for you to know how I came to know the Lord before you see how He led me to use my business for Him. Not only is this a way for you to get to know me a bit, but it is also critical to the story: without trusting Jesus Christ as my personal Savior, there never would be a story of how He led in my life to serve Him.

I grew up in a home where good morals were taught. Through their daily living, my parents taught us right from wrong and modeled how to treat people. My parents did not know the Lord, however, so I didn't know anything about the Bible or Jesus Christ.

Until the age of seventeen, I had never been in a church. I remember thinking, "I wonder what goes on in church?" I also remember wondering what Christmas and Easter were really all about. I knew that they were special religious holidays, but I didn't really know any of the details surrounding them.

In my senior year of high school, I was in charge of the Winter Ball. With all the work of preparing for the event, I procrastinated in asking a girl to be my date. I asked four or five girls, but in each case they had already been asked by someone else. Finally, I asked Nancy, a girl I didn't really know that well, and she replied that she would be glad to go with me. Nancy and I had a wonderful time, and that beginning led to other dates.

A few weeks later, she asked me where I went to church. She was surprised when I told her I had never been to church. At her invitation, I started to go with her to Limerick Chapel in Limerick, Pennsylvania, and in due time, between her witness and the messages at church, Nancy led me to the Lord. I will never forget that summer evening when I realized that I was a sinner and that Jesus Christ paid for my sins on the cross. It was then I asked Him to forgive me of my sins and come into my heart.

The relationship between Nancy and me continued to grow, and we later married, both at the age of nineteen. As I write this (2020), we have been married for forty-four years, have two children and seven grandchildren. It is exciting to realize that the Lord had this all planned from before the beginning of time! What a special blessing to be led to the Lord by my wife and best friend.

The Start of the Business

My father started in the plumbing and heating business back in the 1960s with a pickup truck, a few tools, and a strong work ethic. I still remember him coming home covered with dirt after a long, hard day. As a child I would follow him to the sink and watch all the dirt go down the drain as he washed up for dinner.

One job led to another, and before my dad knew it, his business had outgrown the house. He rented some space from our neighbor across the street. They had a large garage, and Dad used that to store pipe and fittings.

A few more years went by, and his small company purchased land in Perkiomenville, Pennsylvania and built a warehouse and office there. Thus, Perkiomen Valley Plumbing and Heating was born, and at its prime had about forty employees. As a kid I worked around the shop, sweeping the floors, putting fittings and tools away, and doing anything else that needed to be done.

My dad decided to install an in-ground vinyl liner pool in our backyard. He bought a do-it-yourself kit and installed the pool himself. After the pool was installed and running, he couldn't find anyplace nearby that sold pool chemicals. So, he decided to take the space used to park one plumbing and heating truck and make it a retail pool chemical and accessories store. The plumbing and heating office was on the other side of the wall from the pool chemical store. When a customer would come in, a bell rang and Dad or one of his secretaries would take care of the customers. My dad taught me how to cover the store by myself on Saturday mornings until noon. In those days, many stores closed at noon on Saturdays and didn't even consider opening on Sundays. I was only twelve but I enjoyed learning the products and how to take care of people. Of course, Dad was always just a quick phone call away.

I wish America could go back to those days. I realize I can't change society or impose my views on the marketplace, but I can decide how *my* business will run. Our seven retail ski and snowboard shops are not open on Sundays. We place signs in the door and throughout the stores letting people know that we are Christians and believe Sunday is a day of worship and a day to spend with family. We ask that our customers allow us to serve them six days a week.

I became convicted about closing for Sundays back in the early 1980s. When we first made the change, we had customers leaving angry messages on our answering machines telling us how crazy we were to be closed when they wanted to shop. Our non-Christian store managers complained because they thought being closed would affect their sales bonuses. We stayed with our convictions, and now we get messages from customers appreciating our stand. Our employees never saw a loss in their bonuses, and now appreciate the time with their families, away from the business. God has blessed us in honoring Him, and this past season (2019) was our best ever. Store sales are up 5.3 percent and Internet sales are up a whopping 53 percent—only God could do that!

Soon Dad decided to sell swimming pools too, both above-ground and in-ground. He hired a schoolteacher to manage the pool business for him in the summer. The business was very small, but it was large enough to support an employee in the summer. This allowed my dad to concentrate most of his time on the main business, plumbing and heating.

My brother and I started to ski at Spring Mountain, a small ski area near us. I was eleven when I first put on a pair of rental skis and took a few lessons. The skis were wooden with metal screw in edges, and the bindings were cables that went behind the heel of the boot. You pressed down on a handle in front of the toe piece to tighten the cable. During the first lesson, I had a major problem learning how to get up after taking a fall. I thought, "Wow, it's hard to get up with these things on your feet! I won't keep *this* sport up." Well, here I am fifty-two years later, and I still love the sport! (By the way, it really *is* easy to get up once you know how!)

There wasn't any place to buy skis nearby, and the space that sold pool chemicals in the summer was empty in the winter. The schoolteacher who had been managing the pool business in the summers was a skier and talked my dad into using the empty space for ski merchandise. *Result*: Dad decided to sell ski equipment, and he asked that teacher to manage both the pool and the ski businesses.

The initial ski inventory that first year cost $15,000. It is a risk to start a business from scratch and invest that much money in inventory. That amount of money in 1971 equates to about $95,000 today. Fast forward to 2019, when we started our winter season with $10.3 million in inventory. Only the Lord could have known that He was going to bless us in the way He has! He knew from that very first season, when the first skis were placed on display, that in 2020 there would be seven stores in the Philadelphia suburbs and that Buckmans.com would become one of the premier ski- and snowboard-specific Internet sites in the world.

Taught How to Work Hard

And whatsoever ye do, do it heartily, as to the Lord, and not unto men. (Colossians 3:23)

The soul of the sluggard desireth, and hath nothing: but the soul of the diligent shall be made fat. (Proverbs 13:4)

When I was eleven, I would go to work on Saturday mornings with my dad. He would give me tasks that were achievable but also challenging for a young boy. At the time I didn't think they were simple, but looking back now, I realize they were easy tasks. Cleaning up, organizing pipe fittings, washing trucks, and cutting the grass were some of the jobs I would do at the office/warehouse, for $1.35 an hour. During the school year, my mother would take me to the office after school and I would help out. One of the tasks was to add up long lists of costs for pipe fittings for jobs my dad was bidding on. I would double-check his math for the bid lists. Back in those days there wasn't software to compute these automatically. The best way to ensure that a mistake wasn't made was to have me add up the list of materials with an adding machine—the kind with paper tape—to see if I would come up with the same total he did. When our totals didn't match, I would take the tape and double check that I entered the numbers correctly. It was exciting whenever I discovered a math mistake that my dad had made!

When I was fourteen, I worked installing pools in the summer. This is where I learned what hard work really is! Jackhammering rock for the deep end of a pool, shoveling tons of sand into the bottom of the vinyl pool liners and then finishing it off with a trowel before the liner was installed, carrying buckets of cement around the outside bottom of the pool to cement in the walls—these were things that had to be done. It was back-breaking work, but the job had to be completed.

I thank the Lord and my dad for teaching me what hard work is during those teen years. Lessons learned then have stuck with me my entire life. In the 1970s I would work long hours with a starting wage of $5.25 an hour. I don't remember getting time and a half for over forty hours, either! I just worked because that is what my family did. If there was a job to do, I simply had to do it, however long it took. I think the average workweek was about seventy hours, and that never seemed odd to me. To this day I enjoy hard physical work on short-term mission trips. When I say *enjoy*, I mean it: I really like working hard and remembering my formative years of "manual labor." Whatever the job is—mixing cement, carrying block, digging ditches, etc.—and with whatever makeshift tools we have to use in developing countries, I still look forward to getting dirty and tired in the work. This is all based on the fundamentals of old-fashioned hard work, learned when I was a teen.

FROM HIGH SCHOOL TO WORK

I graduated from high school in 1974 and decided to attend Elizabethtown College in Pennsylvania. My college career didn't last long, just one semester and a half. I quit college and went to work for my dad as a plumber during the day, and worked in the pool and ski shop on weeknights and Saturdays.

The pool and ski shop manager gave my dad notice that he was leaving, and my dad asked me to take over managing those businesses. The Lord was at work even then, though I didn't realize it. He was starting to set things up for His greater plan.

In those days, sales were just $46,000 per year, with one part-time employee and me. Now, nearly fifty years later—and only through the Lord's leading—sales are $75 million per year, and we have 450 employees, including part-time staff.

Throughout the years, the Lord has put the puzzle together one piece at a time, knowing that He was going to use the company for His work.

NOT HAVING A COLLEGE DEGREE

For I know the thoughts that I think toward you, saith the LORD, thoughts of peace, and not of evil, to give you an expected end. (Jeremiah 29:11)

Sometimes I wonder what life would have been like if I had gone to college and graduated. Over the years people have asked, "What college did you go to?", assuming that I have a business degree. In these moments I smile inside, knowing that God was directing my life in a different path. Don't get me wrong: I think college is good and I certainly recommend it. For me, though, the Lord had other plans.

God's plans are specific to each person, and they are just right for each individual. Our youth pastor asked me to speak to the teens of our church. He said it is good for them to hear from business leaders and to see how the Lord has led in their lives. I quipped, "You know that I didn't go to college and that I got married at nineteen, right?" I wasn't sure he still would want them to hear from me! Still, he wanted me to go ahead, and I believe it was good for teens to see how the Lord leads each individual in the pathways He knows are just right for that person.

I believe that an integral part of this leading was the important role of my dad. Through him God shaped me and orchestrated the circumstances He intended to use later. The Lord wanted me to learn from my dad during the four years that I would have otherwise spent in college. Little did I know then that he would pass away earlier than I expected. In hindsight, I am convinced that it was the Lord who prompted me to quit college when I did. How I cherish my years in Dad's "college"! Precious, foundation-building years!

By watching and working alongside him, I learned how to carefully watch expenses, to know what the cost of a product is versus what we sell it for, and many other valuable business basics. Beyond the basics, however, I learned that hard work and customer service are keys to success, that every customer is important, and that, in order to grow the business, you need a strong team of employees backing you up—people who embrace the same philosophy.

DAD'S PASSING

And we know that all things work together for good to them that love God, to them who are the called according to his purpose. (Romans 8:28)

I can do all things through Christ which strengtheneth me. (Philippians 4:13)

My father passed away in 1987 at the age of fifty-seven. He left the companies to my brother, sister, and me. I was thirty at the time and felt overwhelmed. Dad had always been there to bounce things off of, to discuss the small and big decisions, and I felt alone without his business skills. My brother and sister were there and gave great support, but it just wasn't the same. I tried to apply Romans 8:28, but I have to admit that, at the time, it was hard to see how the Lord was working this for good. Now as I look back, I can see that even though this hurt terribly, it was good for me to be forced to take charge and run the company.

Within a month after Dad died, the bank canceled our line of credit. "Nothing against you guys," they explained, "but without your father here, we don't feel it is wise to continue the line of credit." I think we had a line of $10,000 then. It was the first test we faced without Dad. We met with other banks and found National Penn Bank that was more than happy to support us with a line of credit. Thus our first crisis was taken care of by the Lord. It was the beginning of many lessons He wanted me to learn. One of those lessons was to trust and depend on the Lord for help in all matters, including business. I started to learn that He cared about the business and was there to guide me through tough times.

The bank that canceled our line of credit has come back a few times over the years asking for our business back. We haven't felt led by the Lord to go back to them, or even to let them make a presentation.

Another crisis came three months after Dad died. Our neighbor filed a complaint with the Township, focused on our packaging of swimming pool chemicals. He claimed we weren't properly zoned for our operations. Hearings were scheduled, and I asked the Lord to give us the wisdom and the words to say. We eventually were given the blessing of the Township and were allowed to continue our business as before. This was another experience of learning the Lord's love for us and His direction. I was learning how God cares about all parts of our lives, including our businesses.

The Lord Grew the Business

Commit thy works unto the LORD, and thy thoughts shall be established. (Proverbs 16:3)

Blessed is the man that walketh not in the counsel of the ungodly, nor standeth in the way of sinners, nor sitteth in the seat of the scornful. But his delight is in the law of the LORD; and in his law doth he meditate day and night. And he shall be like a tree planted by the rivers of water, that bringeth forth his fruit in his season; his leaf also shall not wither; and whatsoever he doeth shall prosper. (Psalm 1:1-3)

As the Lord directed, the company grew. We added ski shops. New pool chemical customers seemed to come out of nowhere! The Lord kept on blessing us, and I began to think of Him as our sales manager. One opportunity after another to grow the business just seemed to "happen." I would get a phone call from a competitor in the ski business, asking me if I wanted to buy their business. Never wanting to close a door that was potentially from the Lord, I would say, "I hadn't planned on it, but let's meet."

After reviewing their business, the owner would name his price. My reply was invariably the same. I reiterated that I hadn't planned on this, but could afford to pay cost minus twenty percent for the old inventory and the appraised value of the building. I could not, however, pay them anything for the good will of their business, that is, for the reputation of the business and the resulting contacts and income potential. I also requested the mailing list, store fixtures, and the store phone number at no additional charge. This happened with six different ski shops, and each of them eventually said, "Fine, let's do this!" It was the Lord leading us to purchase established stores for basically the cost of the inventory, at twenty percent off. Some of these stores had been in business for sixty to seventy years, with hundreds of established customers. This worked for us because people don't line up to buy seasonal businesses. The Lord had this all figured out: He has us postured in two seasonal businesses that are different but complement each other perfectly. Only He could have set this up.

We got out of the retail side of pool chemicals as the Lord led us to sell pool chemicals on a wholesale basis to the pool and water treatment industries. We decided to specialize in a few chemicals that others didn't want to package, and the Lord blessed in major ways. One acquisition after another took place, as one competitor after another would sell out to us. We added warehouse space along with an increasing lineup of trucks.

We now have over forty trucks delivering products in the summer, along with countless third-party trucking companies hauling for us, making deliveries from Maine to Florida and throughout America, east of the Mississippi. Our packaging and warehouse operations are housed in a 210,000 square foot facility.

Around 1998, the Lord directed us to sell ice melt products in the winter to help off-set the growing summer pool products water treatment business. Over the years the sale of ice melt products has grown to be a major part of our business, but it is also the part most highly dependent on the weather. If it doesn't snow, we don't sell any product. When it does snow, the phones ring off the hook!

In 2008 the Lord directed us further to build a manufacturing plant for the main chemical we package and sell, sodium hypochlorite. We had never manufactured anything before, and the Lord taught us many lessons in getting the plant up and running. Currently, the plant produces 30,000 gallons per day.

The Beginning of Using the Business for the Lord

But this I say, he which soweth sparingly shall reap also sparingly; and he which soweth bountifully shall reap also bountifully. Every man according as he purposeth in his heart, so let him give; not grudgingly, or of necessity: for God loveth a cheerful giver. And God is able to make all grace abound toward you; that ye, always having all sufficiency in all things, may abound to every good work. (2 Corinthians 9:6-8)

When my father died we, his children, inherited the businesses together. I knew my brother and sister wouldn't agree to give ten percent or more of company profit to the Lord's work, and this created a giving problem for me. I was one-third owner of the business that they managed, Perkiomen Valley Plumbing and Heating, and likewise only one-third owner of the business that I was managing myself, Buckman's Inc. For this reason I could not give from the companies, not even from the business for which I was responsible.

The Lord had a plan all along, however. In 2001 my brother, sister, and I purchased Spring Mountain Ski Area. The very place where we had learned to ski came up for sale after it had been closed for a year. During the startup of that new venture, for the first time in our family, we experienced business disagreements. It was decided that we should separate the companies. Buckman's, Inc. had grown in size and value, so it was up to me to buy out my sister's and brother's one-third ownership of Buckman's Inc. We agreed upon a value and a time frame, and I paid them for their shares. I also gave over to them my shares of Perkiomen Valley Plumbing and Heating.

At this point the Lord started to show me how this commercial company could be used as a ministry! It was really an exciting time—a new beginning for me as I looked for ways to serve the Lord through the business. Now, for the first time, I could give to the Lord's work directly from the company. He quickly showed me that we could do more than give finances. Giving money was just the beginning of what He had in mind.

The businesses were separated in 2001. At the time of this writing (2020) the company is five times the size it was in 2001! This has all happened by the Lord's blessing and leading the way.

I simply asked Him for direction, help, and wisdom, and He provided just that!

BIBLICAL PRINCIPLES THAT GOD BLESSES

Trust in the LORD with all thine heart; and lean not unto thine own understanding. In all thy ways acknowledge him, and he shall direct thy paths. (Proverbs 3:5-6)

The steps of a good man are ordered by the LORD: and he delighteth in his way. (Psalms 37:23)

GOD'S PLAN, NOT MINE

Sometimes people ask me about my three-year or five-year business plan. I say, "I have no idea, I stopped planning years ago. I just wait for the Lord to show me what is next!" I know this may sound like a poor business model. Sometimes I would prefer to answer that we invest large amounts of time planning for the future of the company or that we have a brilliant list of action items to implement over the next year, the next three years, and the next five years. However, that simply isn't how it has happened.

Here is an example from 2018. In January, we received a notice from a competitor stating that the owners were interested in selling their business. That company delivered pool products to commercial pools and water companies, just as we do. We spent a lot of time looking at the company's details: its volume, where it delivers, how many more employees would be needed to handle the volume, etc. We made them an offer, they countered, we countered back, and we had settlement by the end of March. This added about two million dollars in sales and blended perfectly with our current business. We hadn't planned to do this. We are not on a mission to buy out our competitors. We hadn't even considered it as a possibility until the Lord brought it to us.

Later in 2018, a competitor that packaged five-gallon containers of sodium hypochlorite (as we also do) contacted me about selling that portion of their business. Three weeks later we came to an agreement, adding ten percent more volume annually in this sector of our company.

Still later in 2018, the fastest acquisition in our company history took place. A competing company in northern New Jersey contacted me. They wanted to sell their small bulk sodium hypochlorite business. It turned out they were closing their business and we were able to quickly come to terms on acquiring their customers.

These kinds of things have happened time and time again over the years. Aaaah, but we know that these things don't "just happen." It is the Lord dropping these opportunities into our laps. It is His working and blessing us. There is no other explanation. You might say that our business has been patterned more after the wisdom of Jeremiah 33:3 than that of the Fortune 500.

GOD'S PROVISION

Thine, O LORD, is the greatness, and the power, and the glory, and the victory, and the majesty: for all that is in the heaven and in the earth is thine; thine is the kingdom, O LORD, and thou art exalted as head above all. Both riches and honor come of thee, and thou reignest over all. ... But who am I, and what is my people, that we should be able to offer so willingly after this sort? For all things come of thee, and of thine own have we given thee. (1 Chronicles 29:11-14)

It is hard to think that our company isn't really *ours*. After all, we business owners put in lots of hours building our companies and taking care of seemingly endless problems. King David also put a lot of work into establishing his "business," the nation of Israel. Consider his comments upon giving a massive amount of gold and silver for building the temple in Jerusalem: "Am I something special because I can give something back to God? After all, everything we have comes from God" (paraphrased from 1 Chronicles 29:14).

Let's go back to some basics here. No Christian business owner should forget this principle: anything we have, including our business, is the Lord's. The Lord has given us everything—absolutely everything! Once you realize you are serving Him, and that the Lord of Creation is your boss, a new and transformative reality sets in. He is the one in charge, and you are running the company for Him!

This perspective provides fresh enthusiasm to do an excellent job for Him and for His kingdom. With this new enthusiasm also comes a heightened sense of responsibility. I don't want to mess up and disappoint the Lord! When I die, I don't want to meet Him and find out that I didn't do what He wanted me to do or that I accomplished nothing of eternal significance. When I meet the Lord I want to hear, "Well done, thou good and faithful servant" (Matthew 25:21). Don't miss this point! It is crucial. I continually ask Him for direction, help, and guidance, because He promises to grant these to us if we ask.

EMPLOYEES

Masters, give unto your servants that which is just and equal;
knowing that ye also have a Master in heaven.
(Colossians 4:1)

As a believer, I want to be the best employer my employees have ever had! Isn't that the way it should be? I can't imagine any employer that wouldn't want this to be true, but how much more for a Christian employer! Christ should radiate from us in everything we do, including our relationships with our employees.

One of the most basic jobs of an employer is assigning tasks. How we ask employees to do things is a key to a healthy relationship with them. First, it's *asking* rather than *telling*. You never want to come across as a dictator, barking out orders. It is the marketplace, not the military. Second, asking employees to do significant work is essential to growth. I learned early on that delegating was going to be important if the company was going to grow. Show them how to do something, check up on them, and then let them go and do the task. Nothing is more frustrating to our employees than being criticized for a poor job on something that we didn't train them to do properly. Fail here and negative feelings will flood your workplace.

There was a time in the early 1980s when I thought I had to be involved with everything. I would get to the store or office at 7 a.m., go home for an hour for dinner at 5:30 p.m., then return to work until the store closed at 9 p.m. I was wearing myself out and not being a good husband or father. Something had to change. Someone told me about a simple book, *The One Minute Manager*, by Ken Blanchard and Spencer Johnson. The Lord used this highly practical book to teach me how to delegate! I began implementing the principles I learned and changing the way I operated. Changing our habits is never easy, but this was another way God worked to grow the company. If I had not learned to delegate, the company could have never grown past what I could get done myself.

Encouraging employees is also very important, and I quickly learned that I was to be the chief cheerleader as I led our team onward in their work. I started looking for ways to encourage members of our team. A positive word, a "Thank you," or a sincere and hearty "Good job!"—these go a long way in helping people know that they are appreciated. To this day our management team makes it a point to actively look for employees doing things right. They take the time to send hand-written notes saying how much they appreciate what the employees are doing. My son or I write a P.S. on the cards and include $25 gift card to Wawa (a gas station chain with great sandwiches and snacks). Everyone loves Wawa! I am amazed at how this small gesture provides huge encouragement to the recipients!

I also try to constantly keep an eye out for ways to help our employees in times of need. We send meals to the home if a family member passes away. If the employee is in the hospital, we send a "Get well soon" balloon bouquet. We want our employees to know we care about them sincerely.

We also write a newsletter called *Employee Notes* that we email to our entire employee list. These issues cover current happenings in the company and provide another forum for praising employees who go above and beyond the call of duty.

Recognizing and praising the positives goes a long way with employees, but managers know that we also must deal with negatives. Many would say I am too easy on employees and give too many second chances when an employee has done something wrong. I have had employees lie and steal from us. We have had drivers lose their driver's licenses, and we found other work for them until they could drive again. The list goes on and on. My policy has been to forgive and give a second chance. Christ has forgiven my sins; therefore it seems like a small thing for me to forgive someone for wronging me. Some of these employees who made a mistake, and whom I chose to forgive, now have over thirty years of service with the company. Some of them even run complete departments, with many employees under them.

Of course, I have had to fire employees over the years and those days have been some of my toughest. I wouldn't wish that level of stress upon anyone. A few of these instances were tied to sexual harassment. When an issue like this arises, you must assess the situation and act quickly, realizing that other employees are watching every move you make. Now your Christian testimony is on the line. You *know* what is right and you must *do* what is right.

Don't delay when you know someone has to be fired. There have been a few times when someone wasn't getting the job done. I met with the person; others met with him or her as well. I would procrastinate, thinking things would improve. I remember one event when I finally concluded that the employee was not correcting his actions and showed no evidence of change. I told him that he was fired and that he should collect his personal belongings and leave. He said something like, "What took you so long? I thought this would have come a long time ago!"

All things considered, I am glad that I have been on the side of showing grace and second chances to my employees.

Another employee policy that has worked out well is our practice of hiring believers. Some Christian businessmen I know say they shy away from hiring believers. When I ask why, they say they are concerned that, if things don't work out, it will be hard to let that believer go. Certainly, I can tell you that a few times, "things haven't worked out," but those few occasions are outweighed by hundreds of times when the relationship has worked perfectly!

Most Christians are honest, hard-working people— absolutely the kind you want to work for you! Just make sure when you hire them, they are well qualified for their positions. When I have gotten into cases where things didn't work out, it was usually because I was trying to make it work for them. I hired people to help them out of a tight spot in a time of unemployment, but they were simply not well suited for the tasks they were given.

What a joy it has been to have good, hard-working believers as employees! In providing employment for these families, I have had the privilege of being part of the Lord's work in their lives. What could be better than that, to be the conduit the Lord uses to provide for them! This is a way your company can be used of the Lord as a ministry—as a way of encouragement and meeting the needs of other believers. In a world where business owners are often caricatured as greedy overlords taking advantage of the weak, we can be ministers of God's grace with a humble spirit.

How to Treat Vendors

A good name is rather to be chosen than great riches, and loving favor rather than silver and gold. (Proverbs 22:1)

Your testimony to your vendors also matters. You may never have met them, but believe me, they know you—and probably talk about you. You are either known as someone who is honest and pays the bills or someone who is questionable and irresponsible.

I learned early on that it was important to pay our bills on time. As believers, we should strive to be known for this. Even in the early years of the company when cash flow was tight, I would pay our vendors on time. I wanted to have an excellent reputation with them. And they noticed. There came a time when I asked a vendor for help advertising their products to our customers through a billboard or direct mail. The vendor replied, "Well, we don't usually do that, but since you pay your bills on time, let us see what we can do. You know, most of the ski industry doesn't pay their bills on time, and we appreciate that you do!" This was my first realization that vendors do take notice. Until then I had been naive and thought everyone paid their bills on time. From that point I realized the importance of a good reputation as an excellent testimony for the Lord!

Most of our chemical invoices are due in thirty days, so we post our bills to pay them in twenty-five days. This way the vendor gets the check in thirty days, allowing a few days for the mail to get the check delivered. Our ski and snowboard vendors date their bills based on when the merchandise comes to us. If the merchandise arrives in August, the invoices are due in December or January. We do the same thing here and send the check five days before it is due, so the vendor gets it in time. Now that electronic fund transfers (EFTs) are used more frequently than checks, we have adjusted this pattern by a few days. The point I want to make seems fundamental, but I will emphasize it anyway: *Pay your bills on time!*

Believe me, the simple act of being punctual with your bills will cause your light to shine brightly, because the rest of the world tends to pay their bills late! Your vendors will notice there is something different about you, and that difference is the Lord! This may lead to an opportunity to share Christ when you meet them.

If a vendor accidentally invoices you a price that is too low, or sends you more product than you are being invoiced for, be sure to point this out. You will knock their socks off by telling them! Imagine this response: "Let me get this straight, ... you are calling us to tell us that we invoiced you *too low*?!" Being honest in a dishonest world speaks volumes about who you are and builds integrity for you and your company.

As I write this, we have a classic incident in progress. We buy high-quality salt for our sodium hypochlorite plant and also package it into forty-pound bags of pool salt. The vendor made a huge mistake. The salt comes by boat from The Netherlands to the Port of Delaware. Our contract calls for us to pay for the salt before the ship leaves. The price can be approximately $2,200,000. After the ship arrives, we get a check back for adjustments due to the dollar-to-euro exchange rate and the diesel fuel costs for the ship. All this is written into the agreement.

As it turned out, for this particular shipment the dollar was stronger than expected against the euro and the cost of diesel fuel was very low. We received an email from the vendor stating that our credit back was $480,000. "Wow!" I thought, "This is great." It was a busy time of the year and I didn't have time to work out the credit numbers myself, but I asked our controller to make sure everything was correct. The vendor wired us the money, but a few days later our controller came to me and said that the vendor made a mistake in the credit. The amount we received was $180,000 too high! Knowing how we operate, we smiled at each other and I said, "Have fun making that call back to the vendor letting them know!"

Being honest in your business dealings honors the Lord and of course, integrity is a non-negotiable for any believer in business. But when I told my controller, "Have fun," I meant it! Is there anything more rewarding than representing true Christianity at a time when Christians are so often misunderstood and misrepresented by the media? When such opportunities arise in your business dealings (and they will), *have fun* letting your light shine for the Lord!

Honoring the Lord is the main consideration, but there are side benefits, too. When you need support from your vendor for a lower price, or extended terms, or co-op marketing funds, the vendor will be eager to help you—or at least the vendor will listen to you—because he or she knows that you are honest and that you pay your bills on time. We negotiate hard with our vendors, asking them for extended dating and co-op funds, and we often hear how they want to help us because they know that they can depend on us to pay our bills on time. We receive about $125,000 per year in co-op advertising funds from our ski and snowboard vendors. We ask and they give, partly because they know we pay on time.

Having a reputation for paying on time reaps benefits to the business, but admittedly those benefits are hard to measure in some cases. Regardless, as Christian business owners and individuals, our primary consideration is never the bottom line, but our testimony to Christ.

GIVING AND TAXES

And he said unto them, Render therefore unto Caesar the things which be Caesar's, and unto God the things which be God's. (Luke 20:25)

A Christian businessman once quipped, "I willingly give to Caesar all the things that are Caesar's—but not a dime more!" The less we must pay Caesar, the more we can give to God and provide for our business and employees.

Currently, the U.S. tax code allows charitable giving to be deducted from taxable income. This is a reflection of our great nation's values. Let's hope that this continues! However, this incentive isn't the reason we give; it's just a side benefit.

To be a wise steward of our funds as we give, we make sure that a tax receipt is issued so we can take advantage of this legal provision. Most charities are properly registered to issue tax-deductible receipts, and this in itself provides an extra layer of accountability that they are legitimate organizations making proper use of donations.

There are times, however, when the Lord speaks to you to give but there isn't a way for you to get a tax-deductible receipt. That is fine! Make sure that you give and aren't driven by the tax deduction! This may happen when you are on the mission field. You see a need, and the Lord speaks to your heart to give cash and meet the need right away. It also may happen when you meet someone who has a need and you believe that you should send a financial gift in cash anonymously. The important thing is to give when you are prompted to give—but get a tax receipt whenever you can.

BE A CHRISTIAN FIRST

Let your light so shine before men, that they may see your good works, and glorify your Father which is in heaven.
(Matthew 5:16)

When I meet businesspeople for the first time, I look for ways to communicate that I am a Christian. I also look for indicators that they are believers.

I remember one competitor that we were attempting to buy out. We had several talks, and then they were ready to come and visit our facilities. They asked if they could come late in the morning, and we could bring in sandwiches and work through lunch. I thought, "Great, this creates an opportunity to pray before lunch and to let them know we were believers." Later in the negotiations, the one owner said he was Catholic and he appreciated my praying before the meal. He was in his late sixties and said that in his entire business career, he never had anyone pray before a business meal! Oh, by the way, the deal went through, and we did buy them out.

Another way to give signals about our faith is through the simple objects or decorations on my desk and around our office. For example, I am involved in a missions support avenue called CoffeeHelpingMissions.com. I keep a bag of this coffee on the corner of my desk. People ask questions about it, and that leads naturally to the fact that I am a believer and lets them know where I stand spiritually. I have discovered that many of the folks I do business with are believers like me. This gives us a common bond as we do business together.

Shared faith, however, does not always mean shared values. One time we hired a business consulting firm to analyze our company and make recommendations on how we could run the business better. The consultant would be with us for two weeks. I found out on the first day that he was a believer, so I felt confident that he would understand that we wanted to run our company for Christ—giving generously to His work. After a few days, he advised me to leave my beliefs at church on Sunday and run the company by making only bottom-line decisions for the business. He said that I was holding the company back from making more money, *and that I should leave the company*!

Suffice it to say we were not on the same page spiritually! Considering his approach of prioritizing business before Christ, I kindly asked *him* to leave. I didn't need to be taking advice from someone with that spiritual attitude. There was a silver lining, though. His "advice" spread throughout the company and gave my team an opportunity for some good-natured fun. Laughter is great for employee morale—even if it had to come at my expense!

*Main office and the corporate headquarters
of Buckman's, Inc.*

DETERMINING HOW MUCH TO GIVE

But this I say, He which soweth sparingly shall reap also sparingly; and he which soweth bountifully shall reap also bountifully. (2 Corinthians 9:6)

Give, and it shall be given unto you; good measure, pressed down, and shaken together, and running over, shall men give into your bosom. For with the same measure that ye mete withal it shall be measured to you again. (Luke 6:38)

I view giving as a way to worship the Lord—a way to give back to Him a portion of what He has already given to me. Giving is also the Lord's way of supplying funds for His work. It is truly more blessed to give than to receive! That's right: you are *blessed* when you give—blessed to see souls saved and lives changed, to watch your church move forward, and projects succeed. Imagine! All these things can happen through our giving! The key word here is *through*. It is God who is working, but *through* us. Please don't get me wrong. I am not saying God's hands are tied until we give. If He doesn't supply through us, then He will through someone else. But God has *chosen* to use our giving. What an honor! Without a doubt, it is awesome to give!

If you own a business, you have a responsibility to give both from the income you bring home in your regular paycheck and from the income your company makes.

For us, giving from our home account or salary goes to our local church. At least ten percent is given each week, and, in addition, we give to our church's faith-promise missions fund. These funds are then the responsibility of the church to use as the leadership sees fit, being applied to the ongoing expenses of running a church and supporting the church's missionaries. This amount is given weekly. Not only does the Bible prescribe giving on a weekly basis (1 Corinthians 16:1-2), but this is also important for the church to operate with a stable and predictable flow of income.

If we are away for a week on vacation or for business, we make up the missed giving on the very next Sunday that we are back. It seems to me that when church is canceled, say, for a snowstorm, the next week's offerings should be double. I am amazed that this does not usually happen. It is as though people don't take their giving seriously as a practice or lifestyle of worship to the Lord. If they did, it would show clearly in the next week's offering.

Giving from your business is more complicated than giving from your take-home pay. As I share some experiences and recommend some procedures, I am not saying my method is the only way to give from a business. I am just trying to share what I have done and to commend it to you as something that has worked very well over the years.

On the surface, determining how much to give from your business seems like an elementary task, but I discovered it wasn't as easy as I had thought. When I was first able to give to the Lord from our company, I thought that establishing the ten percent figure would be straightforward. Just take ten percent of the profit and give it to the Lord's work. Each month I read our in-house financial statements and would give ten percent of the monthly profit as the year progressed.

After the year was over, however, our accountant did the books and came back with a number for the profit that was only half of what our in-house statements had indicated. At the same time, we had a cash crunch because of having given so much! Now, this may sound like we had a poor in-house accounting system, but anyone in a small business will know exactly what I am saying here. You really don't know the final profit for a completed year until the accountant's work is done. Depreciation and other expenses have to get worked into those numbers. Now that our company is larger, we have the staff to figure this out more precisely, but back in the early days we simply couldn't afford that kind of staff.

Here is how we operate now: When the accountant finishes the books for a given year and identifies the profit, I establish a giving budget based on ten percent of that amount. It is simple and works well for me. By using the previous year as the basis for this budget, you create a guideline for decisions in the current year. If the Lord directs me to give over and above the ten percent budget, that is fine. He has directed me to do that many times. By identifying the baseline, however, you can plan the current year in light of the fact that you are going beyond the ten percent benchmark.

I set up a simple spreadsheet with the ten percent budget number at the top. As I go through the year and give, I simply record the date, whom the gift was donated to, the amount, and what the project was. It is simple and quick, and provides a record to look back on as the year progresses.

Deciding how much to give is an important first step. After establishing the charitable giving budget of your company, your next challenge is where to direct those funds.

Get ready! *The fun is about to begin.*

WHERE TO GIVE

The steps of a good man are ordered by the LORD: and he delighteth in his way. (Psalm 37:23)

God will set in order your giving, but even in giving, you need to bring sanctified business sense to the table. Start by asking for Expert advice—that is, ask the Lord to direct you, and He will. God's principles are universal, but He also leads us individually, including how to give from our business. God leads many people to direct their business giving toward their churches, in the same way that we give to our churches from our personal income. Generally, the Lord has led me to direct my business giving toward special projects rather than toward regular, long-term giving for the general support of an organization or individual. Some of those special projects have been in my local church, but most have related to missionary projects and Christian organizations. The stories that follow relate to the latter, but you will find principles that apply to your giving however God leads you.

LOCAL CHURCH

In any active, growing church, there are always needs to be funded. I love looking out for special projects at our local church and giving towards them. There have been building programs, computers, video equipment, sound control board equipment, vehicles ... the list goes on and on. When a need comes up, I simply ask the Lord what He wants me to do. Ask the Lord to direct what you should be involved with, and He will direct you indeed.

MISSIONS

You may have noticed that my writing style is intended to be straightforward, as if I were having a personal conversation with you over coffee. If we were in my office or at a coffee shop, I would lean forward at this moment and make sure I had your attention, because *what I have to say next is crucial. Be sure to get this part!* Here goes.

As the Lord put missionary project giving on my heart, He first led me to *get to know many missionaries personally.* This didn't happen overnight. We had missionaries into our home for meals or to stay overnight when they were visiting our church. We would then request to be added to their email update lists. This way, whenever they sent an update about their ministry, we would be empowered to pray for them more specifically. We would also look out for needs in these updates, whether indicated or implied. If you intend to give purposefully, you must *actively look out for the needs!* Then pray about whether you should give toward an identified need and, if so, how much.

Another way to get informed about missionaries' needs is to listen when they give their reports at your local church. Often you will hear of a project this way. Then meet the missionary after the report. Get to know him or her as best you can in a short meeting in the church lobby. Get their prayer card and follow up with an email, asking to be on their email list. This also gives you a method by which to stay in touch with the missionary. After you have prayed about helping to meet the need that was mentioned in the report to the church, you can email the missionary, indicating that the Lord spoke to your heart about giving. Then you can work out the details of how to get the funds to the right place.

Our church has a yearly missions conference, and I attend all the services, meals, and reports. Having many missionaries in one place for a short period of time provides an excellent opportunity to meet them. It is, perhaps, the optimal time for hearing about their needs, seeing their passion, and even getting a sense of how qualified the missionary seems in managing the funds he or she is seeking.

It was precisely in this way that God opened up an incredible opportunity for us. At our annual missions conference our church hosted a meal for the missionaries each evening. The dinner was open to all the church members who wanted to come. I was looking for one of the missionaries to sit with, and the Lord directed me to sit with the conference's keynote speaker. His ministry is in the "closed" countries of the Middle East. This was not long after the USA had gotten into the war in Iraq and Saddam Hussein had fallen.

I asked the missionary if he had any needs, and he shared with me that he was starting the first Baptist church in Baghdad and needed funds to get it started. Wow! An opportunity to help get this church started and to see a Christian work established in the heart of this war-torn Muslim country! Notice the steps here in how the Lord worked:

- I was **looking** for a missionary to sit with.
- I **asked** if there was a need.
- I **prayed** and **considered**.
- The Lord **directed** me to get involved.

In the months that followed, the blessings rolled in. I got to see pictures of people who had been saved and baptized in this church. Certainly the giving helped that ministry, but to say "It was a blessing to *me*" would be an understatement for sure! I repeat, it is more blessed to give than to receive!

The Lord has used our annual missions conference to introduce Nancy and me to many, many missionaries over the years. He has then directed us to help these missionaries with funds for getting their belongings to the field, for the purchase of airline tickets, for vehicles, and for other needs. If your church has a missions conference, don't just *attend*, but *engage*! If your church does not have a missions conference or bring missionaries in regularly, encourage your leaders to do so! If they will not, find another way to engage with missionaries and consider finding a church that loves global missions.

Another way to get to know missionaries is to go on short-term mission trips. You really get to know a missionary family well by spending a week with them. I know what you are thinking: "Can I really get to know someone in a week?" The answer is a resounding *yes*! When you are ministering with them and hanging out with them, you talk about all kinds of things. In the course of everyday interaction or by directly asking, you find out about projects and needs. Then you evaluate and ask the Lord if you should give toward the needs. At the end of the trip, make sure you are on this missionary family's email update list so that you can pray for them and continue to look for future projects or needs. Ask for needs and look for projects, and the Lord will show you where to direct His funds.

The more you get to know missionaries, the more you will be blessed by the relationships formed. Some of my best friends are missionaries. As relationships form, you call or video conference once in a while, and email more often. As a friend, you are available to give advice, which missionaries need. They have many decisions to make and you can be available to help them think through various topics. They are alone in a faraway land, and sometimes they just need someone to talk to. Sure, they have their home church pastor and their mission board for advice, however, missionaries have told me they sometimes need a neutral party to "bounce things off of." Mission boards and pastors are, in a way, their bosses. In my role as a friend, I provide a safe place for them to share ideas.

"In the multitude of counselors" there is both safety and wise planning (Proverbs 11:14, 15:22, 24:6). Pastors and mission boards are invaluable counselors for missionaries. However, the "multitude of counselors" concept expresses the value of gaining various perspectives. As a businessperson, and now as someone older than many of my missionary friends, I think differently, have gained much experience, and can provide a viewpoint that others may not have.

Missionaries don't usually speak of themselves as entrepreneurs, but the more I observe what they actually do, the more I understand how similar their work is to starting and running a small business or international franchise. Before they even begin, they must raise their support. This requires visioneering, marketing, communication, and maintaining an ongoing relationship with their donors. When they get to their fields, they report of having to "wear many hats" as they manage finances, lead teams, and launch their ministries in sometimes hostile and rapidly changing market environments. Do these things resonate with us business owners? Absolutely! As businessmen, the Lord has wired us differently, and we see things through a different set of life experiences. Many missionaries lack experience in business matters and need our help. This is how the body of Christ can function beautifully in missions.

As I write this I recall several practical discussions with missionaries just in the past several months. I talked with a missionary in Greece about renting a property for a future church. Another missionary in Papua New Guinea called to discuss the purchase of a piece of land for a church building site. A missionary from Peru sought counsel on whether he should transition from one ministry to another. A missionary couple in Eastern Europe related to my wife and me the overload they were experiencing in far too many administrative matters, preventing them from having a greater ministry impact, so I floated the idea of hiring someone locally to help them and gave recommendations on how to utilize such an assistant for maximum efficiency.

Offering counsel also brings responsibility. When a missionary asks me, "What do you think?", I don't sugarcoat my answer to match what I think he wants to hear. I seek the Lord's wisdom and tell them frankly what I believe. Our responsibility involves not only speaking the truth, but also diligently seeking God's wisdom. If I don't know about something I just say, "Let me pray about that, and I will get back to you."

One time a missionary discussed with me the problems and possibilities of distributing Bibles in a so-called "closed" country, a place where spreading the Gospel is not allowed. If the people distributing the Bibles were to be apprehended, they would likely be imprisoned or killed. Counterbalancing this grave danger was the thrilling opportunity to get a lot of Bibles into that country and to distribute them to many people. This was a project planned on a major scale. Whatever "*a lot of Bibles*" just evoked in your mind, you are not thinking big enough—I mean ... *a lot!!* When I heard the word "distribution," I thought, "Whoa! That is something I know about!", since my company distributes pool chemicals and ice-melt products (*a lot* of them!). As I considered this Bible distribution project, I found myself asking practical questions about what the quantities would be per day, what would happen when the Bibles reached the distribution point, and what the logistics were. Was the distribution point always the same? How many hours would one trip take? Where would the Bibles be hidden? Etc. These were all questions the missionary would probably have thought of sooner or later, but they flooded my mind intuitively and immediately. Thinking it through together helped the missionary lay out a plan that worked efficiently. It also emphasized to me the need to pray daily for this operation and to pray by name for the people carrying out this dangerous work. The project lasted about one year, if I remember correctly, and it was highly successful—praise the Lord! Just think of the dear people in that closed country being able to read the Word of God for the first time and coming to know Him! Someday in Heaven I will get to meet them! Have I mentioned the word "fun" yet?!

Another time, I received a call from a missionary asking me to pray with him. He needed wisdom about the possibility of moving to another area within the same country. At the time, my friend was about fifty years old and very easily could have finished out his lifetime in the ministry where he was currently serving. It was a well-established work with a large church, a seminary with about 110 students, and a radio ministry. But the Lord was directing him to start a new work. He told me that the new work would be in the capital city where property was very expensive. To buy land there would be like buying property in New York City! Radio was an important part of his ministry, so in addition to property he needed a radio frequency. This meant he needed to buy a radio station along with all the equipment. The estimated cost was $1,500,000. The missionary and I prayed about this move and asked the Lord to provide the funding if it was His will. After a few months, a station came up for sale. The missionary shared the need and opportunity in an update sent out to his email list, and most of the funds came in. As settlement came closer, there was still a need for funds. I prayed about the need and whether we should somehow give more through the donation fund of our business, but I was concerned that if we gave more, our business finances would be in trouble. The deadline grew closer and closer, and the Lord brought another idea to my mind. The company's line of credit had a significant balance of available funds, so I borrowed the needed amount on our line of credit. Then I paid back the loan myself with gifts to the missionary of one-third the amount over three years. Our company could easily afford the one-third payment per year from our giving budget. The Lord used these funds to help the missionary buy the property. Now, a number of years later, the radio station has been on the air reaching over nine million people per year with the Gospel! A church has been started with more than 150 people in attendance. Three other smaller radio stations were recently purchased nearby, reaching even more people! Only God could put these things together.

Remember though—and, again, please pretend that I am leaning forward, coffee in hand, looking you in the eyes, emphasizing this to you—*the key to all this is getting to know missionaries*. Only then will you get to see where the Lord is working and what the needs are. You get to have "a front row seat" to see what the Lord is doing around the world!

Another way to give is through your local church's mission project fund. If your church doesn't have such a fund, meet with your pastor and ask him if he could use a fund like this, distinct from the main budget allotted for regular missionary support. Missionaries have many needs such as vehicles, buildings, computers, cameras, video projectors, drones, emergency flights home for medical needs—the list goes on and on. What a blessing if their supporting churches can help meet these needs! Your pastor is on the front lines, hearing the needs of the missionaries whom your church supports. Pastors love meeting people's needs, so providing funds to meet those needs will be a blessing to him as well as to the missionaries, without a doubt!

CHRISTIAN ORGANIZATIONS

God may direct you to give to Christian organizations. A word of caution is in order. Some people give to organizations without really knowing anything about them. I believe the principle of getting to know people applies to organizations as much as it does to individual missionaries. You should get to know what the organization does and who is running it. This also takes time, but it is important. Ask questions. Get involved and do your due diligence to know just how your funds—the Lord's funds—are being used!

I first learned about Biblical Ministries Worldwide (BMW) through our home church. It is a mission agency with approximately 450 missionaries spread out all over the world. It is the missions board for many of my missionary friends. I did not get to know the organization in a meaningful way, however, until 2005, when I was asked to serve on their board. In this role I got to know much more about the organization and the people directing it.

One of the projects that BMW funds is a yearly field conference, where a group of missionaries ministering in a certain geographic area gather together. The board travels to that region to invest time with the missionaries—a tremendous encouragement to them and to the board as well. One of the pastors on the board speaks daily, and the businessmen of the board share their testimonies. The fellowship time and the shared meals are designed to encourage everyone in the Lord, and missionaries tell us how valuable this time is to their spiritual health. The travel expenses for all the board members and pastors requires funding, so we give toward these expenses throughout the year. We also help some of the board members' wives go to the conference. This consideration honors their wives and encourages these hard-working pastors!

Giving to Biblical Ministries Worldwide brings many benefits. Churches are being started around the world, believers are being encouraged, and souls are being saved through the ministry of BMW. It is definitely an organization the Lord is using to reach the world!

Southland Christian Camp has also given me the opportunity to serve on its board. This has allowed me to get to know the heart of that camp ministry. Again, getting to know the people and the work of any organization is critical in discerning how to give. More than 2,000 teens attend Southland Christian Camp each summer. Each year more than 150 non-Christian teens report coming to know the Lord. Countless lives are changed and people are encouraged in the Lord. During the fall, winter, and spring, various groups attend the camp for special meetings, from family camps to "Wounded Spirits," a conference which equips people to counsel those struggling with PTSD.

Through my close involvement, I learned about another category of people who benefit greatly from camp ministry, a group often overlooked: the camp counselors doing ministry, who experience significant spiritual growth in the course of their work. Many pastors, missionaries, and Christian business owners were once camp counselors! Each summer more than sixty college students serve at the camp for next to nothing in monetary payment. They counsel the teenagers and maintain the grounds and buildings. As they minister for the Lord at summer camp, they *receive blessings* just as they are used of God to *be a blessing* to the young campers. As I have grown to know the people and the work of Southland, I have grown in understanding how to effectively direct some of the giving fund of my business.

I was also on the board of Global Gateway Ministry Partners. This ministry had three main areas of work: church revitalization, Christian education, and religious liberty, all of which are highly significant and much needed. The church-revitalization ministry really caught my eye, as its main initial focus was the revitalization of churches in London, England. There are dozens of churches across greater London with just a few members. Although these churches have existed for decades, many are dying. The following steps provided the general framework of the revitalization process:

- Change the church name or update its branding.

- Have mission groups come from the USA to do maintenance work or renovations on the building. (In most cases nothing has been done to the building in years!)

- Have mission groups come from the States to hand out thousands of invitations to come to the new church.

- Develop the open ground on the church property to provide income for the new pastor. (Each property is different, but imagine having open ground in New York City and then developing it. That is the case in London. Having rental income or a business on the property, perhaps a store or coffee shop, would provide support for the pastor. The ministry is not getting into the land development business. Development is done by an outside firm, with the ministry getting a monthly income from the proceeds.)

- The pastor for the church is a college graduate that signs on for two to three years. He is then trained and encouraged by the staff of Global Gateway Ministry Partners as he pastors the small flock.

The church-property-development phase of this ministry is the part in which I can donate my skills. The Lord has allowed me to be involved in various building projects over the years, and this revitalization of churches excites me. If this works in London, just think of the many, many places around the world where this could also work!

WHERE NOT TO GIVE

Dollars are finite. Even if your business is greatly blessed, there is no way you could give to every worthy cause. Just as you deliberately plan your business, there comes a time when you must develop a coherent giving plan. Seek the Lord's direction here. What are the giving priorities that the Lord wants you to have? To say it in a more foundational way: *What does the Lord want you, His steward, to do with the funds entrusted to you for a little while?*

With nine stores and more than 450 employees, my business gets hundreds of requests to give funds to many worthy organizations such as school bands, sports teams, cheerleaders, police departments, flower clubs, and youth organizations. Even though these are usually good causes, they just are not where we have predetermined to give God's funds from our company. We were spending more than $15,000 a year on these organizations and, worthy as they may be, we decided to stop and redirect this money to missions. We then wrote out an explanation and printed it on company letterhead for our store managers to hand out to people requesting funds. This explanation states simply that, even though we value the individuals and organizations who approach us, we have chosen to direct our charitable giving to missions all over the world. Sure, the people asking for funds are usually disappointed, but I have been amazed at how many of them understand and express their good will that we are giving to important global projects.

WHEN IN DOUBT, GIVE

*Every man according as he purposeth in his heart,
so let him give; not grudgingly, or of necessity: for God
loveth a cheerful giver. (2 Corinthians 9:7)*

There are times when an opportunity arises and you know right away that the Lord wants you to give to that project or need. While you are reading an email or while you are in a phone conversation, the Lord may tell you to commit right then and give. If the Lord is telling you to give, then do it!

The opposite is true, too. You hear about a need but, for whatever reason, you just know that you are not being led to give. You pray about the project, and the answer still comes back to *not* send funds for that project, but rather to save them for another. Heed that voice! Missionaries sometimes say that a lack of funding is a clear indicator that God is shutting a door or moving them in a different direction. With this in mind, if the Lord is leading you against it, but you give anyway (out of sympathy or pride or for any other reason), you may actually be doing a *disservice* to the missionary. Of course, just because you are being led not to support something doesn't mean the project is not God's will, but certainly in the history of the church, far too many resources have been thrown at projects that never had the blessing of God. Your discernment will grow as you study God's Word, meet more missionaries, visit more mission fields, gain more common sense, and acquire more business sense.

Most often, the Lord will direct you whether to give or not either immediately, or after a week or so of prayer. There are times, however, when you don't get a clear answer at all. You pray and you are still unsure. One hour you think "Yes, the Lord wants us to give toward this." Then, an hour later, you are again unsure of what to do, so you pray some more. If the answer isn't a clear "no," I suggest giving toward the project. Simply put, you don't want to meet the Lord and find out that He wanted you to help toward that project, but for whatever reason you didn't. This kind of thing doesn't happen often, but when it does, I just give.

One example of a situation that did not require a time of prayer began with a phone call from a college student. The student is the daughter of some of our missionary friends. We had used frequent flyer miles to get various members of this family to and from the mission field for Christmas, many times. She was very familiar with how we donate frequent flyer miles to help people in ministry.

One day she called me while I was at the office and asked, "Mr. Buckman, do you have frequent flyer miles available for an urgent need? The father of one of my dear friends here at the college just died of a heart attack! She is from Palau. Her father was a deacon at her local church and was a fisherman. He was fishing and dropped over dead!"

I asked, "Where is she now, and when is the funeral?"

"She is in the car with us now, and we are traveling to another friend's home near college to care for her. The funeral is in a few days."

I said, "There isn't time to search for frequent flyer mile flights, and besides, I have recently used all of the frequent flyer miles for other flights. Who can I talk to there that can find a flight, pay for it, and then I can reimburse them for the flight?"

Before long I was talking to the mother at the home where the two students went. That led to a phone call with the college's business manager who told me he had Delta Airlines on the other line, and he just needed my credit card number.

I asked, "Why do you need my number? Just buy the ticket and I will mail you a check."

He said that he didn't have authorization to advance college funds for a ticket!

I replied, "Really? You want me to give you, a perfect stranger, my American Express credit card number with no credit limit, just because you can't find anyone there to buy this dear girl an airline ticket to go to her father's funeral?!"

I finally said I would give the credit card number under two conditions: he was to destroy the number after he purchased the ticket, and he would promise me a phone call from the college president within 48 hours. It seemed obvious that I cared more for their student than they did!

The ticket was purchased but I never received a call from the college president. I did get a call back the next day from the business manager, apologizing for the events of the previous day. Apology accepted.

A few months later I received a package in the mail from this young lady. In the package was a sea turtle, carved from wood, with other gifts from Palau. She included a letter thanking me for getting her home for her father's funeral. It wasn't me that got her home! It was the Lord who made it all happen.

Years later, Nancy and I, along with another couple from Biblical Ministries Worldwide, were visiting Palau and the BMW missionaries there. At church on Sunday I met the daughter along with her mother. They both thanked me again for the ticket and for the love shown to them, even though I didn't know them. I told them that we all can praise the Lord for how He works! After chatting with them, I walked away with tears in my eyes, realizing the details of how God works and how He used me!

Responsibility and Blessing

With great blessing comes great responsibility. The parable of the talents in Matthew 25:14-30 shows us that great blessing comes to us when we faithfully fulfill responsibilities, whether great or small. There is joy in giving when done in the will of God. May the Lord bless you as you seek how to direct the funds with which God has entrusted you.

GIVING TIME AND TALENT

*And he took his staff in his hand, and chose him five smooth
stones out of the brook, and put them in a shepherd's bag
which he had, even in a scrip; and his sling was in his hand:
and he drew near to the Philistine. (1 Samuel 17:40)*

In the moment described in 1 Samuel 17:40, David chose
five smooth stones and went out to face Goliath. This
moment was the bridge between years of preparation and
years of service. By giving David the lonely job of keeping
sheep, God gave him time to develop a skill: proficiency
with the sling. Then God brought David to the Israeli
army encampment, where his skill was needed. This was
a make-or-break moment in his life. David was "but a
youth" (1 Samuel 17:33, 42)—not adequately qualified in
the eyes of many—but he saw a need and accepted the
challenge as from the Lord.

I think we should all be busy using the talents the
Lord has given us. When asked if I would be willing to

serve in some area, my response is usually: "Let me pray about it and get back to you." I then do just that: I ask the Lord what He wants me to do. Sometimes, like I suppose David might have done and like Moses surely did, I find myself asking, "Lord, others are more qualified than I am; why do you want *me* to do this?"

ONE STEP AT A TIME

I have taken on ministries and areas of responsibility for which I did not feel qualified, but I was sure that the Lord wanted me to accept the tasks. He has consistently shown me what to do every step of the way. I think the Lord tests us to see if we are willing to serve. I don't want to fail these tests, or to hear when I get to Heaven, "Jeff, I wanted you to do this thing or to serve in that area." The important thing is to be willing and then to ask God what to do and how best to serve Him!

The church where I came to know the Lord was a Bible church with both a deacon board and an elder board. I was asked to serve on the deacon board in my late twenties. Just a few years later, when I was thirty, I was asked to serve on the elder board, where I was placed in charge of the Missions Committee. I had an interest in missions before this, but the Lord used this committee to allow me to get to know more missionaries.

When I was forty-four, we moved our membership to a Baptist church, and I resigned the elder board of the Bible church I had attended since I was seventeen. The

Baptist church has a deacon board, and within two years I
was asked to be a deacon at our new church. Even though
I had been a deacon and an elder previously, I remember wondering again, "Lord, am I really qualified to be a
deacon?" After some time in prayer, however, it became
evident that He indeed wanted me to serve that way. At
the time of this writing, I am still serving as a deacon.

"You Guys Think Differently Than We Do"

As mentioned in the previous chapter, when I was for-
ty-six, I was asked to serve on the board of Biblical
Ministries Worldwide (BMW). I remember going to my
first meeting at their Atlanta headquarters thinking, "I'm
no expert in missions. I need to ask them why they want
a businessman." I found out that they like to have three
or four businessmen on the board, serving alongside
eight or nine pastors, making up a board of twelve. I
asked them point-blank, "Why do you want businessmen on the board?" The answer has stuck with me to this
day: "*You guys think differently than we do.* You apply
common sense to your business, and that is what we
need for Biblical Ministries Worldwide."

Being on the BMW board has allowed me to meet
many new missionaries. I have gone to their mission
fields and, in many cases, have helped them with projects. These experiences have allowed me to give input to
the BMW Finance Committee over the years, and now I
am the chairman of that committee.

I became involved with the BMW board with fear and a sense of being under-qualified, just as I did with the church boards. However, God is the one who has made it work out, and these opportunities have been tremendous blessings in my life. Meeting missionaries all over the world and serving with a truly great group of godly men has surely been a highlight in my life. Yes, attending the meetings has required a time commitment. We usually meet two times a year in Atlanta for three days each, and each year we have a field conference, which can take up to two weeks. But I must say it has been well worth the time!

At 57, I was asked to serve on the board of Southland Christian Camp. I had to ask the Lord yet again, "What do I know about camp?". I had never worked at a camp. I had never even attended camp! I wish I had, but all I knew about camp was what my children told me. Before I committed to this opportunity, Nancy and I went to visit the camp. The facilities were good, and the program and the attitude of everyone involved was fantastic! Teens were getting saved, and others who already knew the Lord were making commitments to honor the Lord with their lives. In one of the services, almost all the teens came forward to pray with a counselor for salvation or to dedicate their lives to the Lord! I then realized that serving on this board would be just like serving on the BMW board. I would work alongside other businessmen and a group of pastors. I was there to apply those "business common sense" principles to the camp board! The time commitment was three days a year and a few phone calls, so the Lord led me to accept and serve.

I am also on a few missionary advisory boards. One of these serves a missionary to the deaf. The other serves a missionary who works with a few different ministries, including a ministry to restricted access countries. For the missionary to the deaf, there are six of us who meet in my conference room every four to five months for a 6 a.m. meeting lasting one hour and a half. We give advice on a variety of topics to help promote the ministry. The missionary who is serving in restricted access countries sets up a conference call twice a year to review his ministry and to ask for advice. Additionally, once every two or three years we meet for a day to review direction and to advise.

Other missionaries know that I am available for advice at any time as needed. Sometimes I get an email asking, "When can we talk?". Or my phone just rings, and the questions follow. Other times I have a Skype call scheduled, and the conversation usually begins with, "Jeff, what do you think about... [imagine here some visionary idea for the advance of the Gospel]?". Sometimes my day gets totally interrupted and I don't get anything else done—that is, I don't accomplish my plan for the day. Then I realize that I actually did accomplish precisely what the Lord wanted for that day, which included listening to and giving advice to a missionary who needed someone right then. What could be better than that!

It is important to point out here that, just like getting to know missionaries, getting involved with this sort of "time-and-talent" ministry doesn't happen overnight. These things take time, and they grow in accordance with the proportion that you get involved.

I also want to say that I am blessed with an awesome team at Buckman's Inc. They cover all the bases with excellence when I am away or when a phone call from the mission field changes my plans. I praise the Lord for them because, without them, I simply wouldn't be able to do the ministry things I get to do!

COFFEE HELPING MISSIONS

Let me tell you a story about a relatively new business that only the Lord could have orchestrated, an endeavor born with one mission—raising funds for missions and Christian camps. The product? Coffee! Americans drink approximately 3.5 billion pounds of coffee per year.[1] Big companies cash in on our national love of—or need for—coffee. Tapping into this market solely for the Lord's work has been one of my favorite projects as a businessman. How did God lead us to this?

The General Director of Biblical Ministries World-wide, Paul Seger, had just returned from visiting missionaries in Indonesia. The Lord used a comment he mentioned in casual conversation. I heard him say, "Someone should figure out how to make money for missions by selling coffee. There must be a profit in coffee, because the beans in Indonesia cost only $3 per bag, but by the time they are sold here in the States, the same bag costs $12!"

As you might imagine, being a businessman and a lover of missions (and coffee), that got my wheels turning. Was Paul on to something here? Churches are full of coffee drinkers (I will resist calling them "addicts")! The United States imports more than four billion dollars' worth of coffee per year, and Americans drink approximately 400 million cups of coffee per day.[2] I wondered if money really could be made for missions. My experience had been with skis, snowboards, and chemicals, not coffee, but my mind immediately raced into "business mode," applying applicable questions about supply chains, packaging, marketing, distribution, and bottom lines. I met with a few businesses that roast raw coffee beans in preparation for sale. I proposed that I would provide a private-label bag, supply the beans, and pay their business a per-pound fee for roasting and fulfilling orders. Would any profit be left for missions?

The answer was the same at all the roasting companies: YES! I then selected a roasting company called Twin Valley Coffee, a small, family-run company that takes their coffee roasting very seriously. And they are believers! The result was thirteen geographic sources for the coffee beans. We also have three flavors to choose from. It is some of the best coffee the world has to offer!

The next step was to form a separate company, which we simply called Coffee Helping Missions. For the website I contacted the people who designed our ski and snowboard site, Buckmans.com. A site was designed with the memorable domain name CoffeeHelpingMissions.com, where we emphasize that 100% of the profit from coffee sales will go to missionary projects. People can pick the particular Biblical Ministries Worldwide missionary they want to support, then choose the coffee they want to buy.

One last thing needed to be done: to create a short video (less than two minutes) explaining how people can support their missionary friends just by buying the coffee they would ordinarily buy somewhere else. Missionaries can easily send this video to their sending churches and to the people on their email lists.

At the time of this writing, the site had raised nearly $80,000 for BMW missionaries! Half of the money goes to the missionary whom the customer chooses, and the other half goes to the work of a Bible translator in Indonesia, where the seed of this vision began. Employees at Buckman's Inc. supply the accounting, customer service, and other behind-the-scenes administration as part of their Buckman's Inc. job, allowing all the profit to go to missions.

I had the pleasure of visiting that Bible translator in Indonesia, learning more about his work. I asked him how much of his work would be accomplished if Coffee Helping Missions funds were not raised. He hesitated for a few seconds and asked, "Hasn't anyone told you? CHM is paying *for the entire project*. A local employee was hired to help and puts in sixty hours per week. Twelve part-time locals from one of the villages help with final quality checks of the translation." My heart was full of joy, but he continued: "Fuel to get to the villages, food while the team is in the villages, even transportation by helicopter to the most remote villages—all these are supported by CHM. Whenever a book of the Bible is finished, it is loaded onto a Bible app developed just for this translation project. Even though the people who speak this language live in remote areas, 85% of the villagers have phones that can access the Bible app!"

Only God can set these things in motion to provide His Word to these people in remote areas. And to think, all this comes about just by drinking some of the best coffee on the planet, right here in the United States! One of my missionary friends calls this deal "a no-brainer"!

TRANS WORLD RADIO, ETHNOS360, CHRISTIAN CAMPS

In 2017 the idea of helping missions through coffee expanded greatly. Trans World Radio is a missionary radio outreach whose motto is "Speaking Hope to the World." They engage millions with biblical truth in 190 countries and in 275+ languages.[3] They loved the idea of using coffee to support ministry, so we copied our Coffee Helping Missions model and now they too are receiving support, via the website CoffeeHelpingTWR.com.

Another missions agency soon followed suit. Ethnos360, formerly known as New Tribes Missions, was founded with a powerful vision:

By unflinching determination we hazard our lives and gamble all for Christ until we have reached the last tribe, regardless of where that tribe might be.[4]

The motto of Ethnos360 is "a thriving church for every people," so they chose CoffeeForThrivingChurches.com as their domain name.

Also in 2017, CoffeeHelpingCamps.com was launched to further the work of Christian camps. At the time of this writing, twenty-five camps are being supported.

It is my goal to have our websites raise a combined $50,000 per year for missions and Christian camps. The potential is much greater if people grasp the simple vision that by simply drinking coffee—the coffee they would buy anyway, even from companies that aggressively fund causes Christians do not agree with—they could be helping to spread the Gospel all over the world.

We have sufficient data showing that if just fifty families would buy their coffee through one of our sites, $1,500 per year would be raised for missions and camps. Just imagine if we saw God provide 5,000 new customers dedicating their coffee drinking to the Lord. That would raise $150,000 for missions and Christian camps each year. With so many people drinking coffee every day, it is our prayer that the Lord will use this tool in a powerful way to fund His work around the world.

Of course, we know we can't pull this off with substandard coffee. The coffee must not only *do* good, but it must *be* good! Since we are serving the Lord with this endeavor, we wanted to make sure our coffee is an awesome product. That's why we offer such a wide variety of blends and flavors from all over the world, from plain darks to fancy gourmets, so people can find a perfect match to their likings. Shipping is free to the lower forty-eight States for orders of $40 or more. Our promotional videos emphasize that this is a "win, win" situation, so please inform your friends, churches, and coffee shops that if they drink or sell coffee and love the Lord, they can further His work by choosing this delicious coffee that is helping reach the world with the Gospel.

MINISTRY MILES

In 2002 I was invited to visit a ski manufacture's factory in Europe. Representatives from some twenty-five ski shops were invited. The manufacturer paid for my flight to go, and I noticed that one shop's representative flew first class on our flight from the USA to Europe. I asked him how many skis he buys to get such royal treatment. He said that he didn't buy any more than I did. He simply used his frequent flyer miles to upgrade his seat. He went on to say that he builds up frequent flyer miles by paying for his inventory with credit cards. I immediately thought, "Wow, I could do the same thing and give frequent flyer miles away to missionaries and pastors! I could call them *ministry miles!*"

When I arrived home from the trip, I asked our accounts payable manager to contact all our vendors and ask them if we could pay by credit card. If they said we could, we then asked if we could have a two-percent discount if we continued paying by check. (The two-percent fee is also what the vendor has to pay the credit card company.) Very few vendors agreed to give us a two-percent discount, but many of them said, "Sure, you can pay by credit card."

In the early years of doing this, we needed many credit cards to have enough credit to pay our bills using this method. As I recall, at one period of time we had twenty-six credit cards! As time went by, we built up enough credit with a few companies that we could get rid of most of the credit cards and keep just a few. Now we are down to just six credit card companies, each with a high credit line to cover our monthly purchases. Of course, we pay off each card in full each month so that we don't accrue finance charges and to keep our excellent credit rating intact.

Praise the Lord, we are able to get 200 to 250 frequent flyer tickets per year for missionaries, pastors, and my family just by using credit cards to purchase inventory we need anyway. The Lord has used this to be a blessing to many people over the years. One way we use these "ministry miles" is for the children of missionaries, while these young people are attending college in the States. With this help, these college students can join their families during the Christmas break. Missionary kids are known as "third-culture kids," neither fully "American" nor fully "foreign," and therefore can have a hard time adjusting. Statistics show that the transition from the mission field to life in America is precarious for them—and even more difficult for their parents who are oceans away.

One missionary told me with tears in her eyes, "Jeff, thank you for providing the ticket for our son to join us for Christmas break in South Africa."

I said, "Praise the Lord. I'm glad to help."

She placed her hand over mine and said, "You don't understand how precious it has been to our family to have him home! I am not sure we would have been able to stay on the mission field without seeing him!"

There are many examples of these "ministry miles" being used to help and encourage missionaries. While in Vanuatu on a mission trip, I met a couple who were going to be married. He was from New Zealand and she was from the States. He had never met her parents and didn't have the funds to go to the States to meet them. Ministry miles took care of that. Ministry miles also took care of his parents coming to the States for the wedding. Her father is the pastor of a small church, and he and his wife had never been to Vanuatu, where the young couple was serving. Ministry miles flew her parents to visit and to speak in the churches there.

Another way we use the ministry miles is for pastors to travel to mission fields and hold special meetings. With this help, pastors can encourage the ministries they visit in foreign lands, such as the Philippines, Australia, South America, Africa, and Europe. Ministry miles have also been used for pastors and their wives to get away to relax and recharge their batteries, strengthening them for further service for the Lord! Pastors are on the go all the time and never really get a chance to unplug and unwind. Providing these tickets has allowed them to do just that.

TIME SHARE POINTS

We have a timeshare that allows us to gift our share points to others. We have used this as another way for pastors to be refreshed. Sometimes I hear pastors say they have a special anniversary coming up, so I ask them, "What are you planning?" or "Where are you going?" The answer might come back that they don't know, or that funds are tight, etc. I will then ask them where they would like to go if I could provide frequent flyer miles and a place for them to stay with our timeshare points. You just have to ask and listen, and the opportunities will show themselves to you! Sending pastors and their wives to Kauai, Maui, Florida, Colorado, and on cruises are just a few of the special privileges we have had in this regard.

UTAH AND THE POCONOS

The Lord has blessed us with a townhouse in Utah in the Deer Valley ski area and a cabin on Lake Wallenpaupack in Pennsylvania's Pocono Mountains. We rent out the house in Utah from December 1 to April 15 and from June 1 through September 15 for income to meet the association fees and expenses. During the spring and fall we open it up for missionaries and pastors to use as a place to get away and relax. It sleeps twelve, so it is a good place for family reunions. Sometimes a couple may go and spend time together, away from their busy ministry schedule. The house gets used eighty percent of the time in the spring and summer, providing a place to rest and recharge.

One married couple staying at our house in Utah heard that we were coming there on the day they were leaving. They asked to meet us for lunch. They told us it was their fortieth wedding anniversary trip and how thankful they were to be able to use our townhouse for this special occasion. They went on to say that this was their first vacation in their forty years of marriage, adding that it wouldn't have happened if we hadn't provided the house! God's servants need places to go. All we have to do is keep our ears open for opportunities to help.

The cabin in the Pocono Mountains is near our home just outside Philadelphia. The whole family uses it: Nancy and I, as well as our children and grandchildren. When we aren't using it, we open it up for missionaries and pastors to use. The scheduling can get interesting, because we try to make the calendar work for everyone!

To make things easier to manage, we have a cleaning service refresh each home after people leave. We pass on the cleaning fee to the missionaries and pastors, which they are more than willing to pay. Some missionaries have even told us that, without being able to contribute at least something, they would feel reluctant to accept our offer or to ask for help in the future, since they don't like to impose.

HOUSING FOR MISSIONARIES ON FURLOUGH

A few years ago, we bought a fifty-seven-acre farm next to our business. We only wanted half the property, to give the business room to grow in the future. The owner wouldn't sell just half, however, so the Lord directed us to buy all of the land and then sell half. On the half we wanted to sell, there is a double-wide modular house. Just after we settled, our pastor asked if a missionary family coming home on furlough could use the house.

We agreed and the church supplied donated furniture. This provided a nice home for the missionary family.

About that same time, a house adjacent to another section of our property came up for sale. This house is situated next to our employee parking. Since we have employees coming and going at all hours of the night, we thought we should buy the house and rent it out. If our employees' car lights affect the tenants, that would be easier to resolve than having neighbors who own the house and who might complain to the township government. So we bought the house.

Just after settlement, our pastor asked if we had another place for another one of our missionaries who was coming home on furlough. Well, perhaps by now you know what we did! We said that we had just bought a house next to us and that the missionaries were welcome to use it. For two years we used the house for missionaries, until our church no longer needed extra space for missionaries. This wasn't a problem for us because we viewed it as an opportunity from the Lord—His way to provide for these missionaries. We covered their electricity, heat, cable and Internet. Furlough expenses in the United States often exceed the missionaries' budgets, since they are calculated to meet their expenses on the mission field, so it is our goal for missionaries to live here expense free, and our delight if they can save some money while they are here in the States.

You need to be creative, always looking for ways to be used of the Lord. When you honor God's special workers, He then rewards you for being a blessing to them!

YOUR PRODUCTS AND SERVICES

Serve the LORD with gladness: come before his presence with singing. (Psalms 100:2)

So far in this book we have shared several ideas for giving, but don't forget the obvious: your products and services. Years ago, we began offering our swimming pool and ice-melt products at a discount to Christian camps with pools and to churches needing to melt ice and snow from their parking lots. Later, we were able to offer them for cost, and now we can provide these products free of charge, supplying whatever these ministries need. It is a way we can encourage and help support them with the products they need. We can't afford to do this for every church and Christian camp in our Tri-State area, but we seek the Lord's guidance on how many ministries we can take on. So far God has laid six ministries on our hearts for this kind of giving.

You might not be able to offer products and services for free, but you can at least take one small step. The point is this: help as much as you can. If you have a small business, as we did, offer a discount. Then, as the Lord leads, offer your products and services for cost. Then take on one ministry at a time and donate the goods or services to it. Your business isn't yours. It's God's, and you should be looking for ways to help and serve in any way you can.

REALIZING IT IS THE LORD'S

The earth is the LORD'S, and the fullness thereof; the world, and they that dwell therein. (Psalm 24:1)

In the beginning God created the heaven and the earth. (Genesis 1:1)

For who maketh thee to differ from another? And what hast thou that thou didst not receive? Now if thou didst receive it, why dost thou glory, as if thou hadst not received it? (1 Corinthians 4:7)

Some people may wonder why I let missionaries and pastors use our homes and frequent flyer miles, or why I provide products for free. It is simple: everything I have is the Lord's and He has trusted me to manage these things for Him. Those who have devoted their lives to ministry are often pulled in many directions. For them to be able to get away, to spend time with their families, and simply to rest, is key for their ministries.

Sure, it takes time to plan their flights and to schedule the logistics of who is going to be in what house and when. Yes, we take a loss on the products we donate. However, when we realize we are serving the Lord with products and places that He owns anyway, it isn't hard at all. Our things aren't ours and your things aren't yours; they are His. Again, I urge you to view these things in light of eternity. Do you want to meet the Lord and find out that you didn't properly manage what He blessed you with? I don't! He has directed me to serve Him in this way, so I must!

An eternal perspective—the thought of meeting the Lord—can motivate you to get started with a lifestyle of giving. But I can assure you from experience that you will also be blessed right here on earth, every step of the way. Nancy and I have discovered that sharing our blessings with those in Christian work multiplies our own joy. This can be true for you too.

PRAY, LISTEN, ASK, ACT

Ask, and it shall be given you; seek, and ye shall find; knock, and it shall be opened unto you. (Matthew 7:7)

And this is the confidence that we have in him, that, if we ask any thing according to his will, he heareth us. (1 John 5:14)

Pray and ask the Lord how you can serve Him through your business—through the products you sell or the services you offer. He will show you how to be creative in helping missionaries, pastors, and ministries. Be on the lookout for needs you may be able to meet. Listen intentionally when pastors and missionaries speak. Tune in to general conversations with an intuitive ear, and the Lord will use your listening as a way to speak to you about how you can be a blessing. Ask your pastor and missionaries how they are doing and if they have any needs. Explain what you do in your business and ask if your products or services could help them. As you pray, listen, and ask, it won't be long before the Lord will show you how you can get involved in His work!

If the Lord can use a supplier of swimming pool chemicals, water treatment chemicals, ice melt products, and ski and snowboard products, then He can use your company to serve His work as well!

Sometimes while I am praying, the Lord will burden my heart to give funds to a particular missionary or ministry. One of those times, the Lord led me very specifically to send $2,000 to my missionary friend on the island of Vanuatu. He hadn't made any requests in his prayer letters and I hadn't heard of any needs; I just knew that I should send him the money. A few weeks later, he emailed me and mentioned that he had been with a group of pastors from various parts of the island. They had hiked to an unreached village together and made contact. When his time with these pastors neared its end, he reached into his pocket and gave the pastors all the cash he had. As far as he knew, his account was empty, and he wasn't sure how he was going to care for his wife and children when he returned home. Shortly after getting home, he checked his account and the $2,000 was there. He had given all that he had, and the Lord provided ten times what he had given!

Something similar happened with another missionary couple who are friends of ours. Nancy and I were having coffee with them and the missionary wife said, "Will you pray along with us for help for the ministry?

I am afraid my husband simply can't do everything by himself any longer." We prayed for about a year for help, but still the Lord hadn't supplied anyone. The Lord placed it on my heart to send this missionary $5,000. I didn't know of a need—only that the Lord was telling me to send the funds. A while later I got an email from this missionary mentioning how just the right person had come forth to help in the ministry. My friends had met with his prospective assistant and hired her, not knowing where the funds would come from. When they checked their monthly donations list, they noticed the $5,000 in their account. This amount provided an 18-month salary for this assistant in that third-world country!

Pray. Listen. Ask. Act!

INFLUENCING OTHERS

Whether therefore ye eat, or drink, or whatsoever ye do, do all to the glory of God. (1 Corinthians 10:31)

People are watching you more than you know! They see you on Sundays and Wednesdays at church. Somehow they hear about your involvement in helping missionaries and pastors. You can give discreetly, and we try our best to do so, but let's be realistic: word travels! I really don't know how people hear, but they do. If your motive in giving is to receive the praise of men, or if you manipulate your giving so everyone will surely know about it, you are in a dangerous spot—just ask Ananias and Sapphira! They weren't judged because they gave too little or too much, or because their giving leaked to the public, or even because they spoke about it to others, but rather because their *hearts* were proud and deceptive! So be careful and guard your heart, but remember that there is also an upside when people observe your lifestyle of giving: *influencing others to give!*

I met with a few college guys from church who wanted to ask me some questions about being in business. We discussed various topics, then one of them mentioned how he had watched me for years and wanted to be just like me when he got older and had his own business. The reality of this influence was sobering. Our church has a Christian school. In the school's yearbook, I saw this question: "Who is a Christian leader you want to be like?". One of the students named me! I had never had a conversation with this young man. I barely knew his name; yet, somehow, I had been an influence in his life.

I had the opportunity to speak at Bob Jones University to students majoring in business. They like to bring in speakers "from the real world" to talk nuts and bolts and demonstrate how theory can be made practical. I spoke on how a business can be used of the Lord as a ministry, mentioning some of the specific things that are now in this book. I received a letter from one of the students the next week mentioning how much he enjoyed the class. He had recently asked the Lord how he could be used in business as a shining light for the Lord. When I spoke to his class, the Lord gave him a tangible model of how we are doing just that—serving the Lord with our business.

I thank the Lord for these mentoring opportunities. I understand more and more how contagious the joy of giving can be, so I embrace any chance the Lord gives me to brag on His divine plan of working *through* His people. I bring it up here only to remind you that you will influence others more than you may ever realize. People are watching you and you will influence others by your actions!

NANCY

Who can find a virtuous woman? For her price is far above rubies. (Proverbs 31:10)

My wife, Nancy, covers just about everything at home, and her skills allow me to concentrate on the business and ministry topics. This may seem like a small thing, but it is far from it! Not having to deal with home tasks frees me up to think about, and work on, all kinds of ideas. Nancy is a go-getter. When she sees a need at home, she jumps right in and gets it done. From scheduling for the heater to be cleaned, to raking the leaves, to getting her car serviced, and everything in between, Nancy is on it. She handles our household finances as well, and I never need to worry about what she is doing. Growing up in a home where she had very little, Nancy knows how to be frugal and wise. When there is a major financial decision to be made, we make it together. We have a team approach to what we do, and we work very well together. Without Nancy's diligence and excellent home management, I simply wouldn't be able to do what I do. Nancy is a key reason why so much ministry gets accomplished!

Most evenings I spend a little time at home—perhaps an hour or an hour and a half—working on a mission trip, getting ready for a meeting, writing emails, or thinking through a project. This regular investment of time helps me to keep projects moving along.

Nancy is also one of my business advisors. I bounce all kinds of ideas off of her to get her opinion. Dinner is often a time to discuss business and ministry issues. She never minds hearing about how the business is doing or what the latest events are. It is good to talk things through with my best friend and confidant. Sometimes just by talking about a topic, the right direction becomes clearer. This is our usual routine.

There are times, however, when our routine gets rocked. Since we are involved in two seasonal businesses, our work takes off whenever the weather hits. This often means long hours. In response to a phone call, I may have to stay late at work. It might be two o'clock in the morning and the phone rings—a burglar alarm is going off at one of our stores! When it snows, I need to be on site. This sometimes means that Nancy must deal with clearing our home driveway. She has always been supportive of these business-related interruptions to our family life. Sometimes one of our packaging lines gets behind, and we have to run an extra shift in the evenings. If we are scrambling to find people to help, Nancy comes in to help package product. She is always willing to help. Not only does her cheerful attitude encourage me during a seasonal crunch time, but also encourages our team. If any of our new hires imagines that the boss must have a *diva* for a wife, they realize quickly that Nancy is a *doer* who can outwork some of our hardest working employees!

Because of all Nancy does, I have more time to do ministry-related work. I also appreciate her going with me on mission trips each year. She encourages the missionaries by her love for children, by helping with meals, and by her diligent effort on the work projects. Missionaries love her! They are drawn to her positive outlook. They trust her. They confide in her. I couldn't possibly handle all our ministry outreaches without Nancy propping me up behind the scenes, being with me through thick and thin, and helping us stay focused on the mission—both at home and abroad.

CHAPTER 5 REFERENCES:

[1] *https://www.statista.com/statistics/804271/domestic-coffee-consumption-in-the-us/ (accessed July 22, 2020): "Coffee consumption in the United States amounted to nearly 26.5 million 60-kilogram bags in the 2018/2019 fiscal year."*

[2] *http://www.e-importz.com/coffee-statistics.php (accessed July 22, 2020).*

[3] *https://www.twr.org/who-we-are (accessed July 22, 2020).*

[4] *Brown Gold magazine, Issue 1, May 1943, quoted on the mission's website, https://ethnos360.org/about (accessed July 22, 2020).*

MISSIONS TRIPS

And he said unto them, Go ye into all the world, and preach
the gospel to every creature. (Mark 16:15)

I organize and lead one or two mission trips a year
through our local church, Valley Forge Baptist. These
can be building trips or trips to hold vacation Bible
schools for children—or both! To date I have led nearly
thirty of these trips, taking us to many cities and villages in Alaska, Albania, Aruba, Bonaire, Canada, Costa
Rica, Dominican Republic, England (London), Germany,
Greece, Guam, Hong Kong, Mexico, Palau, Papua New
Guinea, Peru, Puerto Rico, Scotland, Senegal, Vanuatu
and Uruguay.

The benefits of these trips are manifold. First, they
show missionaries that you and your church care for
them. Oftentimes, they feel isolated, as if they are serving the Lord all alone on the mission field. Just showing
up to help them and their ministry gives them a much-
needed boost.

Second, our teams encourage the local believers as they serve with them side-by-side. It shows these believers that we care for them, as well. Deep friendships are formed. I know what you are thinking—how can friendships with people from other countries form in only a week? It will amaze you, but they do!

A third benefit is that the team members deepen their relationships with one another. When you travel and work in ministry together—building something or working with children for a week—you really get to know your teammates. This leads to friendships at church that last a lifetime.

Missions trips also ensure that church members will get to know missionaries personally and pray for them more intelligently. We discover that after these trips, whenever those missionaries share a prayer request, the entire team that went responds by praying like never before, because they know those missionaries so well!

I have developed relationships with some really awesome missionaries all over the world. These are top-notch people, serving the Lord with all they have. It is inspirational to see them at work and to get to know them. The Lord also uses these relationships for me to know where to give some of His funds. I get to know the missionary and his work, and then when he has a need for a project, the Lord uses that relationship to direct me to give.

Mission trips have been critical in my involvement with missionaries and giving. I cannot recommend mission trips strongly enough as a way for you to get involved with missionaries!

What a blessing it is to see these ministries in other parts of the world! I love being in places where, even though I don't know the language, I recognize the hymns being sung in church. It is very special for me to meditate on the message of the hymn as I observe the joy of the Lord radiating from other believers. One thing is for sure, there are believers all over the world serving the Lord!

This kind of experience is especially meaningful in areas of the world with great poverty, such as Peru, Albania, Senegal, and the village tribes in Vanuatu and Papua New Guinea. I enjoy watching the children in these places playing with sticks and rocks with as much enthusiasm (or more) than American kids playing with their expensive gadgets.

I observed this in Papua New Guinea, far out in a jungle village. A boy around ten years old was playing a game hitting a round rock and then rolling it along very skillfully with a stick. In Vanuatu, I will never forget playing a game with young children using old coconut halves and a deflated kickball. Here in the States, that dead kickball would have been tossed out years ago! The people in many parts of the world have nothing materially, but how unforgettable to see their creative energy and to see the Lord shining through them in worship!

We plan mission trips about one year out, first by identifying the needs of the missionaries supported by

Missions trips: installing sewer line in Albania (2006); working a Vacation Bible School in Alaska (2019); building in Peru, with Jeff & Nancy's son Brad (2007)

Missions building trips: Dominican Republic (2018) and France (2019)

our church. Then we form teams to meet those needs. A few days into one trip to a remote part of the world, the missionary asked if a few of us business guys could meet that evening to discuss some difficulties he was having in the ministry. Part of the ministry was a Bible college, and the college was in terrible financial troubles. We stayed up late that evening assessing the situation. We then made some recommendations as the week went along.

Before we left, I mentioned that, if he wanted, we could meet by video conference via Skype or WhatsApp, if he ever wanted to review anything. With a smile he took me up on it, asking if we could meet, along with other business guys from the trip, every Monday evening! We have a standing meeting with four or five team members just to discuss various ministry topics with this missionary. Schedule conflicts come up for us all, but we do manage to meet at least two Monday evenings per month.

Recently the missionary told us that the Bible college would have closed if we hadn't gotten involved and made the recommendations for change when we did. Wow! Was the Lord in that mission trip and its timing, or what?! Praise the Lord for how He works!

On another mission trip to the jungles of Vanuatu, the missionary asked me to give a seminar on how to make money with the resources the locals had in their area. The day before the seminar he sent runners to nearby villages announcing there was going to be a seminar on this topic. Approximately forty native people came and listened intently for more than two and a half hours. I gave a devotional on the parable of the talents (Matthew 25) and then discussed what they had to raise and sell. I gave them the idea of raising pigs and selling them in town, about a two-hour drive away on rough roads. Each pig would bring in $250 and could be raised on garbage and coconuts. They had never thought of this!

They asked great questions on giving and how to do basic math to figure out the Biblical concept of tithing. They also raised the issue of whether they should continue growing a crop if they kept losing money on it. They had been growing peanuts and hadn't made money on it for decades, but kept growing it because their fathers and grandfathers had done so. I encouraged them to stop giving their time to peanuts and to switch to something they could sell for a profit. Basic business skills that we take for granted can be life changing for them.

I am told that some cultures hesitate to modify an inherited family business, such as growing peanuts, to avoid dishonoring their forefathers, or at least creating that impression among their peers. But when a foreign "expert" comes in and advises it for the good of the village, it can change the dynamic and shift the peer pressure. My missionary friend in Vanuatu said that the villagers were talking about "that business guy" and the ideas he shared for months after we left.

As fulfilling as it is to see God use our business skills on missions trips, there are some risks and cultural differences to navigate. We explain to our teams that the missionaries know what is best for us and for their ministries, and that our posture should be as guests, not know-it-alls. We are in their environment and they know how to be effective in their part of the world, even how to *survive*. I instruct our teams that we should always listen carefully and do *exactly* as the missionaries say, even if we don't understand all the reasoning behind it. Failure to do this can bring terrible consequences.

I had a near-death experience on one of our mission trips to Vanuatu. A day or so after we arrived, a cyclone hit the islands with strong wind and heavy rain. As we went to bed that evening, the missionary told us to sleep in our clothes and to be ready to head for higher ground if we heard him banging on pots and pans. Well, I slept through the night just fine without the "pots and pans" alarm.

After the cyclone, however, we headed deep into the jungle to minister at a village, where there is a Bible college training locals to be pastors. We traveled two and a half hours over rough roads, riding in the backs of pickup trucks. Then we hiked for another two hours, crossing rivers as we went. The rivers were getting higher because of all of the rain from the cyclone. We had just one more river to cross before we reached our destination village.

The students from the Bible college came to the river to meet us. We were on one side of the river, the students on the other. The river was now raging before us, at flood stage. The missionary said, "Leave your backpacks on the riverbank and cross the river two by two, holding each other's arms. The Bible students will get your packs." Since I was the trip leader, Nancy and I were some of the first to cross the river, which was at waist to chest height—and we did so with ease. We felt pretty good about ourselves at this point.

I stood on the other side watching the Bible students carrying not only our backpacks but our food as well. I thought, "It was easy crossing the river. I should help these guys out, so they don't think we Americans are wimps." Here I went against my own rule, however, to *always* listen to and *follow* the missionaries' instructions! I started to go back across the river by myself.

Halfway across the river I lost my footing, and the river started to carry me away. Being in pretty good shape and a strong swimmer, I thought, "Just swim to the side, and all will be fine." I swam for all I was worth and looked up. Lo and behold, I was still in the middle of the river—moving further away from the group fast. I tried again, swimming even harder, but nothing changed, except now I was exhausted—and still in the middle of the river!

I thought, "Just try and stand up"—only to be knocked over and tumbled onto the river's rocky floor and thrown around like a rag doll. If you have ever been to the ocean and been thrown around by large waves, out of control and hitting the ocean floor, that is what this felt like. I was worn out and thought, "So maybe this is how I will enter Heaven." Somehow my body discovered a boulder that felt a little larger than a basketball. As I held onto the boulder, I could just keep my mouth and nose above the water that was rushing by my head.

The missionary was running—no, he was *sprinting*—down the shoreline and rushed in to grab my arm and pull me out. I sat recovering on the side of the river, gasping for breath and thanking the Lord for the boulder and the missionary's help! Then the missionary told me that just a few hundred yards farther, the river made a turn to the right and completely disappeared into large rocks the size of dump trucks. I would have hit the rocks and been pulled down among them by the water flow. Most likely, he said, the team would never have even found my body.

Lesson learned? On mission trips, *obey the missionaries' rules!*

A Witch Doctor for an Uncle

Remember how I said you have to actively look for opportunities to serve the Lord? Well, sometimes opportunities just "fall into your lap," especially while on missions trips. I want to share a few of these.

Nancy & I were traveling with the board of Biblical Ministries Worldwide to a third-world, so-called "closed-to-the-Gospel" country, and we met a girl whose uncle was a witch doctor. I will not mention her real name or the country to protect her and the other believers in the region, but let's call her "Debbie."

Here's what happened. We were all in a remote village visiting the home of a believer where a new church would be starting in a few months. The home could barely hold our group of fifteen or so. The kitchen had a dirt floor and an outhouse off to the one end of the kitchen.

Debbie was introduced as the daughter living in the home. I would guess she was about twenty-five years old. She had an open wound just below her knee, with puss weeping from it. I couldn't look at her wound long as it was really gross—even the leg bone was visible!—and I didn't want her to feel like we were all staring at her! Debbie hobbled around on crutches as the family made room for us. She then told us the story of how she was injured. A year and a half before, she had been the victim of a motorcycle hit-and-run accident. The doctors in the area did their best but her leg was still oozing from infection! Debbie's uncle is the local witch doctor and he couldn't help her, which was no surprise!

One of the other board members asked me if we could help financially to get Debbie medical care. He knew of some contacts in the USA and perhaps we could fly her to the States for treatment. Well, God had this all worked out! A believer in the States contacted another believer who knew someone else and, before long, the details all came together.

Debbie would fly with her mother to a hospital in another country, not the USA, but nearer to her country. She would stay in an apartment when she wasn't in the hospital getting treatment. Debbie's mother returned quickly to her village because she was scared to stay in the apartment on the 8th floor! Can you imagine going from a village to a modern city for the first time?! It is probably as strange and scary as going for the first time from a modern city to a village with dirt floors and outhouses!

In the hospital, the infection was treated and then an operation was done. Rehab followed, then she underwent a second operation. Infection set in again and was treated, with more rehab after that. Buckman's Inc. had the blessing of helping with the finances of the flights, hospital care, apartment, food, etc. We sensed strongly that this was the right thing to do.

The local pastor told me that if Debbie returned healed, everyone in the village would view this as "Her God did this!" and would then start coming to church! Of course, "Uncle Witch Doctor" would not be very happy about that! He proclaimed that if she left the village, the treatment would not work and she would die! He even forbade her to go!

Well, God was at work taking care of Debbie. After being in the hospital's care for eleven months, Debbie finally returned to her village, completely healed from the hit and run incident. I just know God will use this in a mighty way, perhaps by removing the spiritual darkness that this and other witch doctors have cast on their villages. As I write, I am not sure exactly how the Lord is going to work through this, but we can't wait to see all God will continue to do.

GIVING THE GIFT OF SIGHT

Spiritual blindness, like the kind in the village I just described, is thick all over the world. The primary work of missionaries is preaching the Lord Jesus who will remove this blindness (2 Corinthians 4:3–6). Of course, Jesus also healed physical blindness and other illnesses. We may not have that kind of power and authority, but we can minister healing and show the love of Christ in tangible ways. Opportunities for this often present themselves on missions trips.

I recall Vanuatu again. We were out in the jungle, about two and a half hours away from the nearest town. We were in a village of about 1,000 people that has grass huts, with many of the men wearing only loincloths. Think of pictures from *National Geographic* magazine! We were there for a VBS children's program, building a pavilion type church and also training local pastors.

I noticed there was a man who would come every day to the pastor training sessions. He was about twenty years old. It seemed he was blind, but at other times it seemed he could see a little. No one had to lead him along as he walked, but he squinted painfully. I asked our missionary friend if he knew him. He did. He told me, "He isn't blind, but he has albinism." His eyes are very light colored and are affected by the sunshine.

Well, it took me just seconds to take off my Oakley sunglasses and give them to him. Immediately he stopped squinting and smiled like I had never seen anyone smile before!!! He could finally open his eyes fully to see in the daylight. That made me smile, too, and makes me think about the joy Jesus must have felt to open the eyes of the blind. I learned later that this man had come for the pastor training sessions, because he wants to be a pastor in a local village. When I heard that, I smiled even more!

I gave him the protective bag to keep the sunglasses from getting scratched, and I can only imagine he takes better care of his Oakleys then I do mine. This is just another small way you can help others and find opportunities while on missions trips—in this case a pastor in training.

I have discovered that if we continually tune in to what God is doing around us, He will continually bless us with new opportunities.

YOU GIVE, HE GIVES

Give, and it shall be given unto you; good measure, pressed down, and shaken together, and running over, shall men give into your bosom. For with the same measure that ye mete withal it shall be measured to you again. (Luke 6:38)

There are two equal and opposite errors when reading a verse like Luke 6:38: *abusing it* and *not using it.*

First, therefore, I want to make clear that I am *not* teaching a "prosperity gospel," that is, the idea that our faith guarantees health and wealth in this life. This false teaching claims that if you want to prosper, simply give to the Lord's work and—*voilà!*—the good life is yours! The error here is in thinking we can manipulate God, using our *giving* as a means of *getting.* That is not what I am saying.

On the other hand, Jesus did say "Give, and it shall be given unto you." There are certainly eternal implications to that promise, but I have also experienced it in this life. As I have given, the Lord has blessed abundantly! But here is the key: The goal is not to give so I can *get*, but so I can *give* (see James 4:1-3).

God's abundant blessing has been evident in my life. I was reluctant to approach this topic, but I believe the Lord wants me to present this also, simply as part of what He has chosen to do for His glory. As we give, He gives much more back to us!

There was a time when I thought it would be nice if the Lord allowed me to give a certain amount per year. The amount seemed like a challenging goal, but nonetheless a goal to strive for. The Lord supplied! We reached that challenging goal in what seemed like a very short amount of time. Praise the Lord!

Okay, I thought, let's double that amount as a "dream goal" and—*would you believe it?*—the Lord blessed and allowed us to surpass that amount, as well!

A few years later another idea began to brew in my heart: Could the Lord bless us with giving more than five times the original amount set years ago? Really, could that ever be possible?

Perhaps you are seeing a pattern here! And yes, the Lord blessed that new idea and has supplied in ways we never dreamed of. I don't feel at peace to share the numbers here, but suffice it to say God has allowed us to give more than we ever could have ever imagined. We praise the Lord for how He has worked!

Let me reiterate: I never welcome a thought in my head to make more money for the sake of making more money.

My goal is to make more money to give more to God's work. That is the mindset I encourage you to embrace. From my understanding of Scripture and my experience, I believe that if you fulfill your responsibility to give from what he has already blessed you with, He is going to entrust you with more to give.

The act of getting is a *channel*. We *get* in order to *give*.

The act of giving is a *privilege*. *We get to give!*

Think of it, the God of the universe allows us to invest in His amazing initiatives all over the world. He supplies needs *through* us!

What matters is a heart attitude fixed on giving, not on getting. The Bible talks about a spiritual *gift* of giving, but giving is not just for those with this gift. Everyone should give! Exercising your gift of giving, if you have it, or simply fulfilling your responsibility to give, brings so much joy and satisfaction that you start *wanting* to give more. Giving becomes what you do. It drives you to make more to give more. It reminds me of what the household of Stephanas must have felt, being "*addicted* to the ministry of the saints" (1 Corinthians 16:15).

Years ago, a relative asked me, "Isn't the business big enough? Why do you want to see the business get bigger and have more headaches and responsibility?" I never thought of the growth of the business as creating more responsibility and headaches. My thought was this: the larger the business, the more we can give to God's work.

The Lord has given us one acquisition after another to grow the company, enabling us to give more. When a new opportunity for an acquisition comes along, I first decide if it is the Lord's will for us to do it or not. I pray about the opportunity as I review the numbers. I then meet with our leadership team and review everything with them, asking for their input, probing for convincing reasons not to proceed. As long as the Lord opens the doors, I continue to go through them.

A few months ago, I was reviewing an acquisition for the chemical side of the business. Everything made perfect sense until we got to the point of needing four more drivers to handle this new business for the summer, because it was already March. We had recently determined we needed to find seven new drivers. That amount was not unusual, but would be a challenge because recent additions to government regulations had created a shortage of qualified drivers. Obtaining just those seven would be a work of the Lord, but if we finalized this acquisition, we would need to find *eleven* new drivers—definitely a work of the Lord! All of this seemed to be a red flag, suggesting that we should abandon the acquisition, but the Lord seemed to be saying, "Trust me! Just trust me on this."

Business common sense indicated that we should not proceed with the acquisition. A shortage of drivers would affect the entire business, jeopardizing the good customer service we were committed to providing for our existing customer base. When I would pray and ask the Lord for wisdom, however, that voice inside of me kept saying to trust the Lord to provide the drivers. I then asked our director of operations, who is a believer, whether he thought we should move forward with the acquisition or not. Without missing a beat he said that the Lord had met our needs in the past and He would this time, too!

When I don't know what to do, I pray and ask the Lord for help. I ask Him for wisdom, which He promises to give (James 1:5). What an awesome thing it is to ask the Creator of the world for help! The Lord can and does lead us personally, but we must also recognize that at times well-meaning Christians have misunderstood the leading of the Lord. That is why I also ask other believers what they think, especially when the issues are more complicated. I welcome their most critical observations. This is what Proverbs 11:4 teaches us: "In the multitude of counselors there is safety."

We proceeded with the acquisition and, within one month, the Lord had provided ten of the eleven new drivers. By the time the season hit in full swing, we had found the eleventh, bringing our total driver team to for-ty-five for that summer season!

The Lord leads and blesses, yes, but please don't use the above example to justify reckless decisions. We must use the business sense the Lord has given us, a sense that can be informed and enhanced by the Word of God and our (and other people's) experience in business. For example, the Lord's provision through an acquisition does not provide additional funds for giving right away. Any bank loan for the acquisition must be paid off. We plan our acquisitions to break even in three years. Once the loan is repaid, then we have more funds to give.

Recently a giving project came up, and Nancy and I had to consider how much we should give. It was a very large project, one that was familiar to both of us. We each prayed and asked the Lord what we should give toward this project. We then shared with each other what the Lord had laid on our hearts. My amount was significantly more than hers, so we prayed some more. A few days later Nancy came to me and said if the Lord had put that amount in my heart, then I should obey the Lord and give it! It was the most we had ever given to any one project—by far. We moved ahead in faith. While we did not presume it would happen, we were not surprised that the next year's profits *more than covered* the amount given. It was our best year of profits in all our forty-seven years of business! We stepped out in faith, and the Lord blessed. Also, in the same year, the Lord provided four new acquisitions within ten months. That had never happened before!

We have a giving God, and He loves to supply us with more than we could ever dream of giving to His work! If you have a heart to give and that is what is driving you, set your business-giving goals high and hang on for the ride!

YOU CAN BE USED
OF THE LORD

Thou shalt surely give him, and thine heart shall not be grieved when thou givest unto him: because that for this thing the LORD thy God shall bless thee in all thy works, and in all that thou puttest thine hand unto. (Deuteronomy 15:10)

If anyone thinks giving generously will hurt or, as this verse puts it, "grieve your heart," I beg you to focus on the rest of the verse: *the LORD thy God shall bless thee!* What a blessing it has been to give to the Lord's work and to be part of what He is doing.

I am humbled to see how God has blessed the ministry of my company and used it to change lives for eternity. I can't explain the blessing it is to hear about souls saved in a ministry we supported, or about small churches we helped to fund and build that now are often packed with visitors. What a joy to see a photograph of a bus we helped to fund, filled with children going to a Christian school, or to get an email from a young woman, years after we were in her town, thanking us for having a teen outreach that affected her life forever. The list goes on and on. People are coming to Christ and believers are learning and being encouraged, literally all over the world! The encouragement to my heart is indescribable.

What a blessing it will be to get to Heaven and learn of all the Lord has done. Even here and now, however, we get to see direct results of our giving and serving. If those fruits bring us joy now, how much more exciting it will be to get to Heaven and see what else God did. Remember the parable of the mustard seed! When He uses a financial gift or an act of service, we might see a few tangible results, but the work of God does not stop there. That person may affect someone else, and so on. Learning someday about the far-reaching, exponential effects of our obedience will be awesome.

One of the ministries we have supported trains and equips pastors, mostly in third world countries. Their teaching program is designed to disciple the trainers so they can reach more pastors and reproduce their efforts as time goes by. Over the years, there have been *tens of thousands of pastors trained.* It is exciting to help with their printing needs, or really any needs they have. To be involved with training this number of God's servants is incredible. God will direct you to these kind of ministries if you are listening and looking for them! As I write this, there are thousands of local pastors receiving much-needed discipling!

Whenever I think about all the things God has done over the years, I smile to remember that He did them through a shy, high school graduate who took over his father's small part-time business. God truly uses the simple-minded people, the weak, and the meek. This makes it obvious that it is God who is at work and it is He who deserves all the credit, certainly not this writer, I can assure you! I love the little verse in 2 Corinthians 4 which says that God uses the weak things of this world so that "the excellency of the power may be of God, and not of us." I want you to grasp that truth, because He can also use you in the exact same way.

As this book nears its end, let me offer some final thoughts. First, I encourage you to work on your business with fresh motivation. Do a "character audit" on your business. Ensure that you have set a good, firm foundation of Christian ethics, and that you are making all your decisions upon that foundation, without compromise. Pay your bills on time. Treat your employees well. In whatever you do, be the best you can be. Then ask the Lord to bless your business with great employees and more customers.

I can't emphasis enough the need to offer incredible customer service. There may be many things that set your business apart from your competition, but customer service is one of the most important ways to do this. It is easy to tout your own business as offering awesome customer service, but remember it is the people who will make up their own minds, as they do business with you. You need to honestly, carefully, and continually evaluate this aspect of your company.

Never forget that you are serving the Lord with your business, and you need to be the very best in your customers' eyes, whatever the industry. For me, it has been selling commodity chemicals and expensive winter toys such as skis, snowboards, accessories and outerwear. Customers can buy these things from many other vendors, but we find ways to offer outstanding service to meet and exceed their needs. If this can be done with chemicals and ski stuff, it can be done with *any* product or service. Keep in your mind one big idea: *you are serving the Lord with your business!* Be good at it and the Lord will show you how to become even better.

As you work on your business, form relationships with missionaries and pastors. These relationships are going to be used of the Lord. This is key, but it is easy to miss with all the pressures at work. Don't miss this! Introduce yourself to missionaries who visit your church. Invite them to your home. Ask about their needs. Maybe God will open doors for you to serve with them on mission trips. You will bless these servants of God and they will bless you. As you reach out, meet needs, keep reaching out, and keep asking how you can help, you will form life-long, life-changing relationships. It is incredible and well worth the investment of time and resources!

We are all on a journey towards eternity, but we all go at different speeds and take different routes. The route I have commended to you in this book is a radical ride of faith. *Hang on!* The ride will be full of blessings as you bless others. Keep this in mind: at the end of the journey we will meet the Lord. I don't want to find out all too late that He had planned much more for me, if only I had listened to Him and gotten more involved. You can serve God, and your business can be part of that. It is an amazing life to live!

WHAT WORKS FOR YOU?

Perhaps you are reading this book but you don't own a business. You may be thinking, "If only I had a business to use for the Lord!" Of course, we all are made with different talents and opportunities. In Exodus 4, God asked Moses what he had in his hand. It was just a shepherd's stick, but it became holy and powerful when it was surrendered to God. Use your life to serve the Lord, and be creative to use whatever "sticks" are in your hand. Look for ways to help missionaries by having them into your home or by giving them gift cards to help with expenses while they travel. Offer to change their oil and rotate their tires when they are at your church. Pray for them on a deeper level by being a prayer partner with them, reading their prayer letters, and meeting needs mentioned in the letters. There are many ways to help missionaries.

Remember, too, that this is not just about foreign missions. Be a help to your church and pastor, too. Actively look for ways to be an encouragement. Many of the things listed above for missionaries apply for your pastor as well. You can clean and do maintenance around the church. Why not offer to babysit so the pastor and his wife can go out on a date? If you are handy with fixing things, offer your services for free for needs in your church or in the pastor's home. Pastors need help, and what an encouragement you will be by helping them in everyday, practical ways. Get creative and you will be blessed.

You certainly don't need to be a business owner to do these things. You may even be retired, like a friend of mine at church, Jim Bowman. Jim is in his mid-seventies and is an usher, serves in our church bookstore, helps the custodial team, is a greeter on Sunday mornings, serves on the security team and does just about anything else he can do around the church. Maybe you are saying, "What can I do? How can I serve?" Just be a "Jim Bowman" in your church! The point is to be busy serving the Lord with the talents and time He has given you. Look for opportunities, be creative, and ask the Lord for ideas. It can be scary to step outside of your comfort zone. Believe me, I know! But what a blessing it is to take that step and later to look back on what the Lord has accomplished!

TO GOD BE THE GLORY

This book has told the story of what God has done in my life, but I want to be very clear: God gets all the glory *for what He has done!* I have just been along for the ride— an exciting ride, I must admit! Don't think it has always been simple, pretty, and easy. No! At times life seemed to be out of control, as if there weren't enough hours in the day to get everything done. Then I would remember, there is always exactly enough time every day to do what God wanted me to do. If I had a problem, it was a priority problem, not a time problem. I was trying to get *my* list of things done, forgetting to focus on what *God* would have me do.

God has directed perfectly every step of the way. It is fun to look back and notice the various pieces of life's puzzle that He arranged at precisely the right times. Each puzzle piece is beautiful on its own, but as more of them get added and connected, the better I understand the big picture. Some of those perfectly placed elements are my meeting Nancy and coming to know the Lord, learning how to work hard, and learning business from Dad before he died. God taught me very early to prioritize customer service, value my employees deeply, and place a high importance on giving. Then God grew my passion for missionaries and their needs, and for serving the Lord on mission fields around the world.

I can't thank and praise the Lord enough for leading in my life the way He has. This book has been just another small puzzle piece, an avenue to invite you to seek what the Lord has in mind for *you*. However he leads you specifically, I promise that life does not get any better than walking with God and serving Him!

DO YOU KNOW THE LORD?

It may be that you are reading this book and don't know the Lord Jesus Christ as your personal Savior. Your very first step in doing anything written in this book is to come to know Him. It isn't enough to accept that Jesus is Lord and Savior. He must be *your* Lord and Savior. I am not talking here about joining a church, getting baptized, "becoming religious" or even giving money. None of those things can make us right with God. This is about understanding the truth about our lives, our sin, and eternal life in Heaven. Please consider these Bible verses:

Our moral condition: "For all have sinned, and come short of the glory of God" (Romans 3:23).

Our plight and our only hope: "For the wages of sin is death; but the gift of God is eternal life through Jesus Christ our Lord" (Romans 6:23).

Our loving Savior and his sacrifice for us: "But God commendeth his love toward us, in that, while we were yet sinners, Christ died for us" (Romans 5:8).

Our responsibility: "If thou shalt confess with thy mouth the Lord Jesus, and shalt believe in thine heart that God hath raised him from the dead, thou shalt be saved" (Romans 10:9).

Our invitation: "For whosoever shall call upon the name of the Lord shall be saved" (Romans 10:13).

You can accept Jesus as your Savior right now. Simply pray from your heart:

Dear God,

You made me and You know me. I admit I am a sinner, and I am sorry. Please forgive me. You gave Your Son Jesus to die in my place, and He rose from the grave. I believe on Him as my substitute. I now accept Jesus as my personal Savior and Lord. Thank you for loving me and preparing a place for me in Heaven. Please help me as I begin my new life as Your child.

In the name of Jesus, amen.

AFTERWORD

By a missionary friend

This part of Jeff's book is a deeply personal history from
the other side of giving. In short, it answers a question:
What is it like to be on the receiving end of mission giving?

We first met Jeff and Nancy almost twenty years ago,
in 2002, when were still basically kids in our early twenties at the very beginning of our missionary journey.
They hosted us in their home in Pennsylvania while pre-
senting our prospective ministry to the former USSR, at
the church they attended. We got along great and totally
loved our stay with them, but we really had no idea that
they gave to missions from their business. We barely had
any idea that they even had a business. I just remember
watching the NBA playoffs with Jeff, eating "real" Philly
cheesesteaks, and thinking, "What a cool guy!"

Several years later, I put out a request to hundreds of
people for assistance with a printing project. We received
one response. It was from Jeff, and it covered the entire
$2,000 needed to purchase the equipment and materials
necessary to start the newspaper outreach. From that

day forward, Jeff stayed personally connected to the growth in our ministry, the strategic plans we had, and prayed with us through the ups and downs that come with global mission work. But what exactly was that first financial request, and what came from it?

In the summer of 2003, after receiving a call in the night from a Christian in Moscow, we were asked to meet with two refugees. After meeting with the two men, we were amazed by their hunger for the Gospel. We met regularly twice a week for several months, culminating in conversion and baptism. Both men read the Bible through in its entirety several times before making professions of faith. After their baptisms, for years, the men and their families met with us regularly two or three times per week to study the Bible, church history, systematic theology, Christian foundations, pastoral theology, and personal evangelism. After years of training, one of the men was ordained to the Gospel ministry.

The men started a Farsi language Christian newspaper, and this is what Jeff's first donation to our ministry enabled. The paper was distributed regularly among the large Afghan communities of Saint Petersburg and Moscow. The Gospel was presented throughout the paper in a spirit of love. Copies were sent by post and courier into Afghanistan and Iran. The response was mostly positive, but it was accompanied with persecution. Both men were threatened, and several beatings occurred. One of the two Afghan men was brutally stabbed on the street and only survived through the intervention of his brother. He was hospitalized for two weeks. We were put on a bounty list with a reward on our lives offered by a extremist businessman in Saint Petersburg.

In the wake of persecution, the ministry continued to grow. When we left Russia in 2006 for furlough, there was a small group of twelve Afghan believers. When we returned in 2007, there were dozens more in a city-wide network of believers! Ultimately three men entered professional ministry, and scores were baptized. A Christian Pashtun language website was built that received thousands of hits per month. One of the original two men went on to do global missionary work. There are now at least three organized groups of believers meeting in Afghanistan as a result of this original outreach.

Many years after the initial donation to launch the printing ministry, Jeff shared with me a very specific prayer request of his own. I passed that request on to the network of Afghan Christians who had been reached through his initial donation. They prayed for him from several different national locations. And yes, the cycle was completed. The impact of the Gospel went to previously unknown places, and the new believers from those places then sent prayers back for the people that helped to reach them in the first place. The Kingdom of God is amazing thing!

The long-term impact of Jeff's original donation led to so much more. The work in Russia led to a region-wide initiative to take the Gospel to places that are impossible or difficult for traditional missionaries to enter. Jeff helped with an extraordinary operation to distribute Christian literature and Bibles inside of Iran. We identified an opportunity to assist a network of pastors in the country with these resources. The problem was that our partnership fell apart with the organization that claimed to have access inside of Iran. The leadership collapsed internally shortly before the operation was to commence. Yet the initial delivery of Bibles had taken place to a holding center just outside of Tbilisi, Georgia. This left us stuck in the North Caucasus with hundreds of boxes of Farsi Bibles and literature. What could we do?

We worked with Jeff and a few other friends from our advisory board. Ultimately, we settled on a plan. Our in-region partners found a transportation partner willing to move the books and Bibles in two shipments using potato boxes as the cover story. It worked! Almost. The shipments arrived to the destination inside of Iran safely. One was picked up. The other was meant to be handed off in a smaller truck at a drop off point in the Tehran area. The receiving party and the driver both got lost, and—for reasons that I will never understand—arranged to meet just off a major square close to the national political buildings. Putting this in American terms, it would be like carrying out an illegal operation just off the National Mall in Washington, DC!

Sure enough, the men, our delivery guys, and the local Christians receiving the materials were all stopped by police. These weren't just any police. These were the special Religious Police of the state of Iran, who just happened to be passing by. Our guys were sure that they were done for. Instead, the police asked them why they had two vehicles stopped in an illegal parking zone. Our guys told them that they were finishing up the delivery of a business deal (which was true – it was Kingdom Business!) and moving the boxes from one truck to the other. The police didn't check a single box! Instead, they told the men to hurry up. They even pitched in with moving the boxes to help clear the area! Every box made it safely into the hands of Iranian Christians.

Some years ago, Jeff started helping with regular giving to support of church revitalization in the UK. At the beginning of this effort, we were working with a single church with four members. This church had not recorded a baptism from conversion since the Second World War! After years of faithful giving, the ministry was able to expand beyond one location and ultimately assist six churches with planting and revitalization. At its height, the ministry had eight different men in pastoral leadership benefiting from Jeff's resources. The ministry established a Bible training institute, and even developed the ability to sponsor missionary visas. More than seventy baptisms from conversion took place across the various locations in about an eight-year period.

What was amazing about London was Jeff's personal willingness to come and serve the main church campus with not just one, but two mission trips. Jeff and his team from Valley Forge Baptist worked to paint, do electric work, tear out old materials, and renovate two different church buildings. Jeff also taught a giving stewardship class for local businessmen in our area. Some of them started coming to church as a result of this class, and two eventually became genuine believers.

The people in the church loved him and his team from Pennsylvania. Many years after the trips, they still talk about "the Americans" who came and changed everything for their little churches. It really is hard to describe all the lives that have been changed through our work as a direct result of the strategic giving from Jeff's ministry. Here are a few more ways that his funds have been used to make a difference: Kurdish Bibles distributed in Syria, church planting in Turkey, ministry training in Egypt, Bible and literature distribution in Ethiopia, leadership training and evangelism in India, Bible distribution in Armenia, Azerbaijan, Estonia, and the Republic of Georgia, pastoral training and church planting in Ukraine and Central Asia, Christian liberty work in Europe, the Middle East, and across the United States, and developing a Gospel preaching network of leaders in Europe. In addition to all of this, Jeff has personally blessed our family at critical moments with "ministry miles" and in other ways, that have allowed us to be refreshed, revived, and sustained. He always seems to know from the Lord just the right time to reach out. The ways and the creativity in which he has blessed so many would take too long to recount. This chapter, and indeed this book, really only scratches the surface. The list truly could go on. The point necessary to emphasize is this: Only eternity will tell the story of what God can do with a team of Christians willing to give together from their time, talent, and treasure. Whatever combination of those three "Ts" that God has blessed you with, the key is to give it to Him, and he will multiply it for eternal purposes that will truly be amazing.

Jeff's giving model is unique because he is unique. He feels and lives the spirit of missions. On one hand, he takes himself out of the picture. Few will ever know the extent of his giving and his compassion for people. On the other hand, he also shows up personally. He goes on trips. He talks to people that he gives to. He listens, gives friendly advice, and lends a helping hand without telling you how to do the work.

It's not our role here to tell you Jeff's process. He lays out his personal giving approach throughout this book. What we can tell you is how it feels to be on the other side. And for us, Jeff and Nancy model Christian faith and Christian missions without layers of religious bureaucracy interfering with the message. They simply show love for God and love for neighbor. In a room filled with mission donors, you would never know which one was Jeff, if you were looking for a stereotype. Instead, you would probably only find him if you were looking for the quietest, meekest, most servant-hearted person in the room (and he won't like me saying that). In a nutshell, that's why his giving is so effective. He doesn't just give. He seeks the Lord's guidance and trusted counsel before he gives. And then, when he gives, he gives without restriction and with the heart of service. Put simply, his giving is an expression of Christian love.

Our partnership in mission began with a simple stay in their home. It soon picked up speed with a single response to an appeal for a computer and printer to publish a newspaper. From there, in an eighteen-year journey to date, it has impacted the four corners of the world.

That's just one missionary story. *What could God do with your business and your story?*

Jeff and Nancy Buckman